THAT ELIXIR CALLED LOVE

RAMTHA

THAT ELIXIR CALLED LOVE

The Truth about Sexual Attraction,
Secret Fantasies, and the Magic of True Love

JZK Publishing
A Division of JZK, Inc.

THAT ELIXIR CALLED LOVE

ISBN # 978-157873-4559

For more information about Ramtha's teachings, contact:
RAMTHA'S SCHOOL OF ENLIGHTENMENT
P.O. Box 1210,
Yelm, WA, 98597 USA
www.ramtha.com

JZK Publishing
A Division of JZK, Inc.
P.O. Box 1210
Yelm, Washington 98597
360.458.5201
800.347.0439
jzkpublishing.com

"In the first place, nothing is so improving to the temper as the study of the beauties, either of poetry, eloquence, music, or painting. They give a certain elegance of sentiment to which the rest of mankind are strangers. The emotions which they excite are soft and tender. They draw off the mind from the hurry of business and interest; cherish reflection; dispose to tranquillity; and produce an agreeable melancholy, which, of all dispositions of the mind, is the best suited to love and friendship."

— David Hume,

Essay I, Of the Delicacy of Taste and Passion

CONTENTS

FIGURES

ACKNOWLEDGMENTS

Our sincere thanks and appreciation to everyone who jointly helped bring about this book. It was an arduous teamwork effort inspired by the same love we all share for our Master Teacher, Ramtha, and his words of wisdom.

We would like to acknowledge Debbie Christie for making the original recordings of Ramtha's words available for transcription. We appreciate the copyediting work of Pat Richker and her zealous dedication in keeping the words of the Master pure. Many thanks to Stephanie Millham for her careful proofreading and professionalism. Special thanks to Jaime Leal-Anaya for the literary edition of this book, the construction of Ramtha's Glossary, the Index, and the essays by way of commentary and introduction to the various chapters of the book.

Finally, we would like to extend our gratitude to JZ Knight for her dedication to the Great Work and for making Ramtha's teachings available to everyone who wants to hear them and explore new vistas of themselves.

PRELUDE
Love, the Blood of Poetry and Beauty

Who does not remember the first time, the anticipated moment of our first passionate kiss? How precious are the memories or the dreams of those innocent times of wild passion. And who has not fantasized in the quiet solitude of their private thoughts about a special love, a unique and magical experience that makes us feel alive and center stage? And yet again, who has not been wronged or disillusioned with a love that could not be or never was?

Love can be such an elusive mystery that escapes us all, that even the greatest poets and dreamers have tried to paint it in words, in dancing strokes, or on stone canvases and failed to capture its face, its features, its turns and straight lines. Even its experience is often so fleeting and short-lived, like water running through our fingers. It is precisely this characteristic that makes it even more desirable, immortal, never fading, still attractive, even when our own life has already been spent and has begun to wither.

The human drama throughout the ages has never tired of seeking this treasure that uncannily seems to be reserved for someone else, as if it were some magic elixir that only belongs to great Goddesses and Gods but never for mere mortals, who fail to hold onto it, grasp it, and know it.

Usually the key to a great mystery or to new knowledge, new paradigms, is hidden precisely at the heart of a paradox. Love is a *mystery* and a *paradox*. Love seems to be a reality beyond the intricacies of our human limitations and personality, a characteristic that would explain why it is so hard to hold onto it continuously or at all in our life. One moment we are in bliss with our lover in our secret, special place — our body rushing with feeling and sensation that is exhilarating and delicious — and shortly after that, once the body has come to a rest and the moment has passed, yesterday's disagreements over silly things find this perfect timing to reintroduce themselves.

Love is a mystery. Love transcends our human nature. It does not show itself as a natural, spontaneous, and generic quality of humanity for as long as we remember in our history. Yet again, what is perplexing and a paradox is our capacity as human beings to conceive and dream of such as love. It transcends our human nature, yet we as humans insist on it and venture through life searching for it. This is the paradox.

I am sure this is the reason why some people have come up with the idea that the best way to describe the divine, God, the Source of all life, is in terms of love. They say, "God is love." Well, we can see why. Love is such an unusual thing. It is so rare, so elusive and mysterious that it is used to describe everything we do not know and understand, those things beyond who we are. Some believers may find comfort in this. But since God is traditionally so beyond who we are, then it follows naturally that love should also be beyond our grasp. Maybe this is one of the reasons why the absence of true, meaningful love in people's lives is so widely accepted as a normal state of affairs. There is a great line in the recent musical movie, *Moulin Rouge!* (Twentieth Century Fox: Nicole Kidman, Ewan McGregor, 2001), between Zidler and Satine, where she tells him how she has finally found true love in her life and he responds to her in bitter sadness, "We are creatures of the underworld; we cannot afford to love." Isn't it so ironic to see that people's most sacred beliefs and perception of themselves — which become an invisible part of cultural traditions — often make them fail to believe in themselves and totally lose hope for the greatest things in life?

We say that love is fleeting and elusive, but is it really, or is it we who are the fickle ones lacking substance? Maybe we have been looking in the wrong direction. Maybe the answer lies within our very self, within the person who often is a stranger to itself, a masquerade of protectiveness who has forgotten who is the one wearing the cloak and the mask in the play.

This book is about exploring these questions and about finding the secret to the paradox of love and discovering something we had missed all along about ourselves. It is a book that allows us to see ourselves reflected in a mirror, vulnerable, under the eye of truth and blatant honesty, wounded by our own hand and lack of knowledge. What is left of our identity, who are we, when all our hidden secrets have been brought out in the open for everyone to see? Would we still be ourselves if we did not need to hide, please, or pretend? What kind of freedom emerges when we love ourselves enough to conquer and know who we are and have the courage to be our greatest potential?

This book is dedicated to all the warriors, poets, and lovers who have wandered through life searching for answers. The journey we are about to undertake in this book is only made possible by the hand of love itself that heals, nurtures, and gives us wings to fly where we have not dared to imagine yet. But love we have not understood. It is the sword of truth that challenges us to conquer our own nemeses that cloud our true indelible nature and pristine identity.

Our host will be an unusual voice that speaks to us from a distant place, yet it is extraordinarily present and aware of our current predicament: Ramtha the Enlightened One, a master

15

conqueror from our own family, who discovered the secret of the ages and now has taken his place among the Gods and Goddesses who hold in their hand the elixir of immortality. Do not dismiss this unusual messenger but consider the thoughts and questions that are offered to us. Consider it a scene, a window, a song that we hear and makes us ponder, smile, and remember.

Consider this: What about sexual love? Why is it such a powerful attraction? Is it right; is it wrong? What about women? What is their true nature, beauty, and value? What about marriage; is it natural or unnatural? They say that animal instinct and attraction is not love, but what about the lessons we learn from the animal kingdom and those rare species that mate for life and are willing to sacrifice themselves for their offspring? What about people who create illnesses for attention so that someone cares for them and loves them once the fire of passion has waned or become tedious and intrusive? Why is adultery often a more thrilling adventure than faithfulness to the partner we say we love? Why is it that many relationships that started in passion and love are tragically reduced to the resentment of having to carry over responsibilities and contractual agreements? How come for some people sex is no longer making love? What are we to do with our sexual fantasies, our secrets that quickly find us the moment our minds start wandering away from our partners? How can we blend love and compassion with powerful strength? Can powerful seduction be a moment of pure passion or does it have to be tainted with scheming manipulation? Can love be an enduring experience?

We will learn that maybe we have been searching for answers in the wrong place. We cannot separate love from its recipient, ourselves. We begin to find some clues when we become sincerely aware of what we really wanted out of the experience. Was our main interest in sexual gratification or something else? How do we see ourselves, as mere body parts, the accidental product of nature, or as something else? Have we resigned ourselves to live for appearances, for someone else's ideals, or do we want to live for something else?

We are all dumbstricken at this point, for we have all had our good share of these experiences. The age-old question still remains unanswered: What is this "something else" you mention exactly?

Ramtha breaks the silence with powerful words, yet graceful and dear, like the sound of a flute melody floating over thundering drums: "That is what all of you are looking for. You are looking for the perfect woman and the perfect man who in your life is irreplaceable."[1]

"You may come to this wonderful realization that when you really become real — real — and just are who you are without playing any game, yes, you are going to have to maybe lose the person who is sharing your bed, but maybe the next person who shares your bed will be your equal. You understand?"

"Truth is freedom and it is also seductive. It is the highest compliment we pay ourself. Our body is not our highest compliment; our mind is."[2]

Love's apparent elusive nature begins to gain color and shape when we change our perspective and turn our attention back to ourselves and see beyond the surface of our façade and body parts. The landscape changes completely when we begin to view ourselves — our highest compliment — as sovereign minds vested with freedom and choices, capable of entertaining

1 *Finding Peace in Love,* Tape 478 ed. (Yelm: Ramtha Dialogues, 2000).
2 *A Teaching Dedicated to the Feminine Gender and Understanding Molecules of Intent and Becoming a Christ,* Tape 374 ed. (Yelm: Ramtha Dialogues, 1998).

an original thought, a new dream that sets the stage and prepares us for the cherished experience to come. We are not merely the accidental recipients of an experience but the mind that contemplated its possibility and made it a reality, consciously or unconsciously.

The confusion arises when we insist on reducing our nature to the bottom rungs of the ladder of human experience: sexual love, needy love, and manipulative love. Life as a human being is much more than these and so is love as well. We have only known three loves out of seven. We have yet to explore unconditional love, the love for truth, love seen in all things, and the forever love of freedom over time and space enjoyed by the true masters who have gone ahead of us and conquered themselves.

Love inspires us to strive for greatness and to see beauty where others only see but ugliness and discontent. It allows our minds to sing and fly with feathered wings and bring to life the promise of a new dream. Love truly is the blood of poetry and beauty. It is the key that clearly shows us we are divine inside, for how can we taste of such an immortal drink that transcends the oceans of space and time and still remain mere mortals? We are more than we can physically touch. We are the mind that animates our body and makes it unique, as elusive and free as love itself.

Having said all of this, now we are ready to begin. Fill your glass with the wine of the Gods, that as surely as the hearts of mortal men and women will continue to be enchanted by this dream for centuries to come, you may also truly come to know *that elixir called love.*

— *Jaime Leal-Anaya*
Writer and Editor, JZK Publishing

CHAPTER 1
Everyone Wants It. Everyone Craves It.
But What Is It?

I am so honored indeed and pleased indeed on such short notice — but what is time? — that you should come and be with me this night. I too have been invited this evening, and I promise you that what you are going to hear tonight will become a great classic in the annals of these teachings in the days to come. So be it. Moreover, what I teach tonight, without sending any runners I will say to you that all of this teaching that you will hear this evening in your time will manifest in your life as a living reality to allow you to engage it or disengage it, as the case may be. So it is not about runners anymore. It is about an intrusion into your reality, an intrusion into your mind. So be it.

You Say, "I Love You." But Do You Love Yourself?

I am coming to the end of my Great Work, and at the end of this Great Work we come to this most precarious four-letter word: love. Everyone wants it. Everyone craves it. Everyone must be sustained by it. Without it there is madness. Without it there is degeneration. Without it there is hope. But if love exists as an invisible angel in our lives and it is free to everyone, we opt to pursue it — people, places, things, times, and events — to find that excelsior feeling, that effervescent feeling, that legendary feeling that is magic, contentment that brings our warring body to peace and our mind to freedom — that is what love does — and to the soul, to contentment. Everyone wants that.

Love is not legendary. It exists in every breath. So to follow up on ancient teachings of this, to say that God knows every number of hairs on your head, knows every breath you have taken, and that should be the supreme example of love, that is absolutely right. That is absolutely correct. But as we grow in our youth we find out how silly this concept is, because we will never find in our minds anyone that will know the numbers of hairs on our head, will never, ever know about us all the concepts that God promises to know about us. We give up on that silly concept. But should we; should we?

In love we come to this great legendary mystery. There is not a person in this audience, neither young nor old, even the most silly of young people and even the most cynical of old, that do not desire to find this magic potion, this potion that we know that if we find this that everything will be right in our mind, in our hearts and soul, in our body and in our kingdom. And with love we find peace, but the kind of peace that doesn't arrest us from life but that arrests us from the past before it was known. It arrests the past and conquers our chains and gives us liberty, a love that allows us a value of truth.

Truth grows in the soil of love. Truth does not grow in the soil of emotions, does not grow in the soil of guilt and shame and ignorance and resentment and jealousy and blame and victimization and doubt. In fact love can never grow from a soil of doubt. All that is fostered in doubt are no answers because doubt provides none. In order to have a doubting mind we are resolved to no wisdom.

Moreover, we know — I know and you know, and if you don't know, you will know; so be it — that love does not bear itself in the poisonous soil of jealousy, envy, suspicion, and mistrust. Love never grows out of that kind of soul, that kind of mind, that kind of soil. Love doesn't grow out of hate, abuse, and self-destruction. Love does not grow — Think of a flower planted in the most acid soil you can imagine. The Dead Sea: The only thing that lives in the Dead Sea is bacteria. No plant, no orchid, no lily, no oak, no great tree grows from a dead sea. Heavy water, the heaviest water on the face of the Earth, is in the Dead Sea — dead sea. Atomic and hydrogen bombs are made from the heavy water of the Dead Sea. Death and destruction comes from heavy water.

Now just as it is with legendary love, it evades you throughout your life because if your mind is upon your resentment, if your mind is upon the past, if your mind is upon jealousy, if your mind is upon mistrust and you are the one fostering that, if your mind is laden in any of these lakes, love — like a rose, like a lily — shall never foster in your life. Does that mean because it doesn't grow in the dead sea of your emotional body that it grows nowhere? No.

Now love, everyone wants. Many of you have resentment toward your parents because they didn't love you. Many of you have resentment towards your past because there was no love. Many of you do have love in your past, and what that was is that you were actually loved into freedom by your parents with a good stewardship that allowed you to know the difference between right and wrong. That is a consummate. You were loved enough to be encouraged to have knowledge. You were loved enough to be encouraged to have freedom in expression. Many of you had those. Then you can say you were loved as a child. Correcting the child does not mean the lack of love; it means bringing right and wrong into an analogical position of discernment. That is a good thing; it is a bad thing; it is a God thing.

Now to find our way to the legend. And the greatest crowning achievement of our life is to know this mystical medicine, and it begins with to love yourself. But if you do not understand love, what does the journey mean? We know that it involves you personally — not your mate, not your children, not your parents — that this message is a mystery, but it involves you, you, you. It is a mystery.

Three Loves Out of Seven:
Sensuality, Suffering, and Manipulative Power

To love yourself. All right, you think you know the definition of yourself, but you do not know the moving verb of love. What does that mean? Well, there are seven steps to this word that we have manifested to some modicum of degree. I did it and you are in the process of doing it.

The pyramid is made up of seven levels, seven bodies, seven consciousnesses, seven fields of life awareness.[1] And so far you came down the ladder but you ain't gone back up yet. So now to love yourself. All right. How many people have you said, "I love you" and have done things to them and thought about them? How many people have you said this word to that you yourself have never said it to yourself?

So on the first seal,[2] how many men and women did you tell them that you love them because you were in lust, and you

---

1 See Fig. B: Seven Levels of Consciousness and Energy, p. 249.
2 The seals are powerful energy centers connected to important glands and organs in the body that facilitate seven major and distinct levels of consciousness. The first three seals are the centers commonly at play in all of the complexities of the human drama. The first seal manifests as sexuality, the second seal as pain and suffering, and the third as power and manipulation. See Fig. A: The Seven Seals, p. 248.

were the predator? You use this magical word to get someone to be seduced by you, give up their intimate, intimate self to give you — this is what you were looking for — mind, soul, and body. The emphasis was on the mind, the programming, and what would follow, the body. "I love you." How many of you told people in your life that you love them because you were on fire with sexual urgency? Raise your hands. Look around. Look around, just so that you know you are not alone; all right? Immediate urgency, that is the thing you pull out. You will pull anything out if you are operating from the first seal. You will pull anything out.

The greatest legend of all is about love; it is the greatest, most magical potion there is. You will bring that out and say to this person that you are in love with them just so you can spill your seed or orgasm or have your way with them. How many of you agree with that? Raise your hands.

Now at the first seal, which is the most politically commercialized selling point in any product, including this school — Sex sells. That is why all those commercials are sexy. That is why in the truth teachings this audience was packed to the gills when it came right down to sex, and I mean sex.

Now so how many of you know that I am scoring so far on this issue of love? Now I want to ask you a question: Would you then dedicate your life, mind, body, and soul to that person that you said that to and they believed you, and you sort of in the heat of passion believed it yourself? Now I want to ask yourself this question: How many of you are happy to know that you were fornicators instead of lovers? Come on. You know, I am sort of seeing a lazy hand going up here. That is good. Now I want to ask you something. Let's pause here. How many of you still are in love with that person, you asked them or you told them that, just so that you in the heat of passion could get it on? How many of you are still in love with them? Wonderful. Why aren't you with them? How many of you are not? So be it.

So we come back to that which is termed indeed where do we find love? Well, first it is an extraordinary, fleeting feeling that happens, but it isn't in our loin that happens. It starts here[3] and it moves to here. This is just reactive, emotional. The first three seals are the animal. They are the animal. They are the territorial, predator — can take down the weakest — procreation. It is the animal part of your nature, which all the animal kingdom is fashioned after. You know, no one made an ostrich until they were that which made the ostrich and then became it. So all nature is made after the consciousness of Gods, and so the consciousness of Gods is made after the first three seals of Gods.[4] So all nature exhibits this "multiply concept without responsibility, without burden." That is the first three seals.

But remember what I taught you about how Tyrannosaurus Rex, how the ostrich, the horse, the bison, the tiger, the lion, the elk, the fish got here: by the Gods who created them. And the Gods who created them breathed life into them. And so what was the life? First-three-seal energy — first-three-seal energy. That is why it is called the animal instinct.

Now the only love in the animal world — except for those animals that mate for life — the only love in the animal world are the mothers who give birth to their offspring and keep them and raise them until they are old enough to fend for themselves. That is it. That is it. So sex is not love. Sex is an animal, basic human instinct, as it is basic with nature. It is basic with bacterium. It is basic with viruses. You know, the

---

3 It starts in the mind first; then the sexual hormones are activated.

4 *Ramtha, A Master's Reflection on the History of Humanity,* Part I, *Human Civilization, Origins and Evolution* (Yelm: JZK Publishing, a division of JZK, Inc., 2017).

next time you ought to, you know, send a valentine card, send it to your old virus. Just a thought.

Now I want to ask you a question, and here is to prove my point. Come on, people. So are you still as passionately in love with these people as you said you were? Would you raise your hands if you are not. So be it. Why? Why did you say you love them? Because that is the magic potion, isn't it?

One of the great teachings I used to teach — I used to — is called "love yourself into life," to love yourself into life. Now love is not just a four-letter word. This may sound corn-doggish to you, with a little mustard, but love is not born in the first seal. How many of you have used your illnesses, have used your body fatigue, your illnesses to garner affection from other people? Now why did you do that? I asked a question, why did you do that? Why did you create this disposition just to get attention? Why? Hey, can I answer that? You did that because the first seal had already worn off and you were moving to the second seal. Does this sound familiar?

Now how many of you again created illness to get the attention that sexual love no longer brought you or you didn't get it anymore? There are more of you, but for now this is truth.

Look at me, my beautiful people. What were you looking for? Love, enough to get sick about, and sometime even to do that to test your own mate, that through your pain and suffering that attention would come but it wouldn't have to come through the first seal, that it would come just from your own sense of self-respect, your own need to find respect in yourself, your own need to find sufficiently that you are greater than your sexual body. How many of you now know you created that flat-out? Flat-out. It is true. Oh, honey, you have got a long way to understand human consciousness. The reason I want you to do that is because healing is in exposition of truth. Healing is in exposition of truth.

Now if you are willing to get sick, if you are willing to feel bad, if you are willing to do this just so you can transfer the energy from your sexual organs to another part of your body to see if you can get it attention, at least that is evolution. That means that there is a great mother lode. That means there is a prima materia. That means that there is a sacredness that you are in search of — you are in search of — because people who tell people they love them, "Lay down, I think you love you" or — No, I forgot how it goes. I will get it right. But a great life is not made on great sex because great sex wanes. It wanes. When the realisticness and the glazedness out of one's eye starts to get clearer and we see what we have done, we are not so attracted any longer to this lie.

But now let us go back to the Holy Grail. What are we all after? Love. What are we all after? Why would we make ourselves sick? To get at least equal attention in our normal life away from the bedroom, we will become ill so as to inabilitate ourselves but to derive the same human touch, affection, and cooing words just to see if we can do it. People get sick because they are sick of being body parts and thinking and brainwashing themselves that this is true love. You will absolutely do it just to see if you are greater or they are greater than the first seal that you magnetized them to you. How many of you understand? So be it.

Now we see the beginning seeds of disease. We see the beginning seeds of madness. We see the beginning seeds of the ending of life, because after the lie has been revealed we don't want to face it so we create accidents, we create disease, we create happenstance, we create trouble so as to keep the attention coming our way, because it was not what was sexually done to us or what we did; it was the hope of love, and we are after the love. Now we are in the second seal — We will absolutely create these things in the second seal of disease and sickness, unhappiness, in pursuit of someone who will understand, that so great is our need that our voice will become louder above the healthy people.

If the first seal is seduction — a man's ejaculation, a woman's gratification — then women who are still living for that sexual gratification from their husbandmen are still struggling with weight. They are struggling with age. They are struggling with everything to keep their bodies looking the way they were when they first had intercourse with this man that said that they love them. Now they don't even — they don't even — hear anything else. They have just got to keep the same moment going. The truth is sex with the same woman, sex with the same man, if that is all you are after, becomes tedious, and then we are into adultery, because if that is the basis of union, it is the very reason for adultery and indeed the very reason for mistrust. Then we move and we take that same energy to the second seal. And so what we start to do are all the things you raised your hands for: illness. All disease happens in second-seal consciousness. All accidents happen in second-seal consciousness. All depletion of body function happens in second-seal consciousness. All disease — let me emphasize it again — happens in second-seal consciousness. Old age happens in second-seal consciousness.

Now since you have been so gratuitous in raising your hands on points of truth, let me tell you something: You are never going to find the Holy Grail in sex. You are never going to find the Holy Grail in disease and mishap. You are never going to find the Holy Grail in the power of resentment, the power of guilt, the power of when you first said "I love you" has now metamorphosized to "that bitch" — don't be appalled; you have thought these things, please — has now in the third seal translated to "You manipulating bastard, you. You told me you loved me. I believed you. I gave you my body. I gave you the best days of my life. You slept with my best friend." I think the next question you should ask is why was this your friend? We should pick and choose our friends wisely. Hey, was I too graphic for you, too graphic?

When it comes to the third seal, love that happened in the first seal translates to child support, spousal support, and bills. I am talking about when the hormones are no longer racing and your mind is now doing cartwheels with fantasies. You are not making love to this man and woman beside you; you are making love to somebody else, or you are watching them do it to someone else, because if you thought about them doing it to you, you would get no feeling off of it. You know why there is such a thing as sexual fantasy and why it has become an operative of naturalness in this society? Because it is a clue that if you thought about the person you are making love to, you wouldn't have the greatest orgasm you are having. And this doesn't speak to everyone, but this speaks to the concept of all those people you said you loved them, and "lay down, I think you love you" or — I still can't get that right. Oh, well. I have learned enough on this plane. So if you have to fantasize about your sexual partner, why don't you just look them in the eye and say, "You know what? I am not making love to you tonight. I am making love to so-and-so," or a thing, and if you did that, that would start you on the road to love.

When Sex Is No Longer Making Love

So we understand that sexual love — sexual love — the first few times is total involvement with the other being, total. That is called sexual love, total involvement; no fantasies, just total involvement. That is sexual love. If you are kinky and you are fantasizing, I mean, you are the one that settled for less. Been there, done that. That is sexual love, when you want somebody so bad you can't wait to bed them. And when you bed them, your mind is crazy with them because all your fantasies — They have been your fantasy; they have occupied your thoughts; they have occupied your emotions. And you finally get them in bed and they get you in bed, and there it is and it is fabulous, so you keep doing it and keep doing it. How about the day that your mind starts to wander a bit? What has happened then? It is no longer sexual love; it is convenience. Yes? How many of you agree? Convenience.

Now how many of you understand so far? What I am asking you is how many of you understand sexual love and when sexual love leaves, when love leaves sexuality and it becomes a habit in which we substitute people, places, things, times, and events? Raise your hands. Can I see that again? I know you were a little hesitant on that, but thank you for your honesty. God bless you. God bless you. God bless you. God bless you. You know why? Because we should always know the intent behind our acts — always. All right. So how many of you have learned something so far?

Now what if you get married to a person because you are sexually in love? How many of you have married people because you were sexually in love with them? All right. For a time they filled the first bill of expectancy, but they didn't fill the rest of those bills, did they?

31

So now we come back to the mystery of the fleeting moment of love in sexuality. Stop eating. You always eat when you get nervous. Stop it; put it away. I am not a television show, and I am talking to you. So be it. Good.

Now then we come to the second seal. Let me tell you something. This may be hard to believe but people actually fantasize about dying and illness to get other people's unabridged attention, and that fantasy is just as strong. Believe it or not — believe it or not, you virile men and women — believe it or not, these people are a level above you in the second seal. I know this is hard, but if your lover gets sick, you should start to go, "Uh-oh, doodie-doodie, doodie-doodie, doodie-doodie, doodie-doodie, do." That means that your lover — your lover — is looking for a greater fulfillment, a greater orgasm. A lover's greatest orgasm is illness in the second seal.

Hey, you all love sex, but think about the powerful adrenaline rush when the person that you love takes care of you and coddles you and nurses you, or that you wish that they would. That is a greater orgasm than sex.

And this little toast is to all of you who now understand — listen — who now understand failing health, psychosomatic diseases, obesity — what is the antithesis of obesity? — skinny, starvation. It is all physical changes, but physical changes only happen because of attitude.

So now here is to make a toast that now we understand that the reason we got ill — "We," I don't know why I keep saying this, and I sound like a Sunday school teacher; I am not a Sunday school teacher, please. The reason you got ill, the reason you had accidents, the reason you crave attention is because it is the next orgasm in line up the seven seals, the seven ladders, to prove true love.

How many of you had fantasies about getting hit by a

car or drowning or being murdered or getting a catastrophic disease and dying so that the partner you shared sex with would somehow fall deeper in love with you at the cost of your own life? How many of you have had those? Raise your hands. Turn around. Look at everybody. Look at your neighbors. Look around. Come on. Look around. I want you to know you are not alone. Look. Look. Look. Look around. Please do. Don't feel alone in this, because if you do, you will think it is special, and it ain't.

How many of you from those days of fantasy have now developed a full-blown disease? Stand up. I asked because your future is standing up. I asked those people who from those fantasies have now developed a full-blown disease. Take a look at what the second-seal need for love absolutely produces in human life. Look at them. Take a look, please. This is not a Fig Newton of anyone's imagination. Turn around. Look at them. These are people now that are wanting miraculous cures. Hey, don't touch your life? Well, you know, from the time I leave to the time you see me again is going to be a space in time, and maybe you are going to join these ranks. So I want you to look, as quiet sentinels to all of your fellow students here, and I want you to see what the need for love unfound in their life has created for them.

You know why they are this way? Because each and every one of you in your own right have told people that you love them just so you could get money from them or you could get shelter from them. You have done that. These are the people who moved to the next level and they got the disease. Not all of them; there are some of them standing up that feel like it is coming on. But I am talking about real disease here.

These people need an extraordinary amount of attention, an extraordinary amount. They need to be loved upon the most fanatical conditions that they have created in their life. Is that possible? Because, you see, if they created this and they lost the people most considered in their life and now they are stuck with their fantasy — are you listening to me? — so now they are looking for love at the end of a fantasy made manifest. Now I cannot explain too much to you the impact of this. Stay standing.

So I want to ask you a question: So all of ye olde disease-free souls sitting down, how do you think you died in your last lifetime? Quiet. You are young now, right, disease-free. Have you ever died? But you can't even imagine it now you are so vital and your bones don't hurt, your muscles don't hurt. I mean, you feel really frisky. So did all these people. So did every one of these people. Hey, you think your lack is not going to catch up with you? Oh, it is going to catch up with you. You know how I know that? Because you died in your last lifetime; then you were born in this one. If you have a birthday, we know you are reincarnated. So be it.

Look at them. These are people who used fantasy to get attention through the diminishing of their own health. And how many of you have done that? Raise your hands. You are next. So be it. You may be seated.

> To the water of life,
> clarity of truth,
> and understanding love.
> So be it.

So love was used to garner your sexual prizes. Love was used when sex, when you became as a spiritual being, began to question if all you were good for was sex — If all your time you were putting it upon your body, why were you putting it on your body? Why were you losing weight? Why were you overeating? Why? Because the emphasis was on sexual gratification.

Lions and Eagles — Lessons From the Animal Kingdom

Every animal and every bacteria has sex. So is it natural? Absolutely. It is not a bad thing; never is a bad thing. But you have come to a spiritual school. You came to a school to be greater than the common people on the street. That is why you invested this time and money and part of your life to study here. Now am I going to tell you that everything they do outside of these walls is the truth? Of course I am going to tell you that, because it is the truth; it is their truth. But you came here and said, "I know people believe this, but I am not satisfied. I have done these things. I have told people I love them and then laughed at myself or queried myself, and I felt bad about it. But I couldn't help myself because I was sexually in lust with this person. It was through them that I got off." I got off; can I make it any more blatant than that? I got off. "I wanted to have sex with them, but I couldn't live with them and they couldn't live with me." This of course is natural. It has always been natural. We were never made unnatural. That is the truth.

We are not bad people because we have sex. That doesn't make us bad people, but it does make us untrustworthy and animalistic and as unprioritized as the animal kingdom. In other words, what that means is that creatures mate; the great stag mates with several does. Those does don't say, "Don't mate with anyone else but me." They all have foals by the stud of the group. But when mating season is over with, all of the does, they live together and raise their young together. It is a selected group. And all of the bucks go off and they live with the men. There are hints of this in your own life. That is very animalistic.

So you argue and say, "Well, all right, Ramtha, if that is the truth that this is natural, then marriage is unnatural." You are right; it is. You are right. You are right. Are there species amongst the animal kingdom that mate for life? Yes, yes. Is that natural? Yes.

What do we do with a great eagle — a great predator, great and massive wings — that finds his beloved and makes love to his beloved and brings her near a river that he can feed her and love her and build a nest with her, and between the two of them they make love? You know why they make love versus the stag and the hind? Because the stag only makes sexual love to the hind but does not love her. That stag will not defend that hind out of season to any predator. He will not save her life and he will not save the life of his children. A lion and a lioness: A lion is part of a pride. And the greatest hunters on the face of the Earth are not men but women. They are the greatest, most violent, most malicious, most clever hunters there are. One lion breeds a pride of lionesses; he breeds them when they get hot. And when they bring down a kill, he is the first to the supper table. Do you want to continue to call him the king of beasts? I think you ought to call his concubines the queen of beasts. And if any woman comes — now here is the stepfather syndrome — if any woman comes to his pride carrying babies from another line, he will kill them. And how many children have been abused by their stepfathers? Raise your hands. Raise your hands. How many of you have lived under stepfathers and have been psychologically or physically abused by them? Raise your hands. That is called the animal world. And the first object is that he kills them or runs them away and separates them from the mother. And he stays with her as long as she is in heat, but the moment she is not in heat, he is off to someone else.

Well, in the animal kingdom they have learned to adjust. They go back to their sisters, their best friends, and the sisters hang together. And the old men, they hang together as long as they don't have to fight over a woman. But will lions in the same pride, a male lion fight another male lion over a woman? Absolutely. And why? Why? Because she is in heat she is going to bear his offspring. He cannot tolerate her offspring from another lion. He will kill them. That is absolute jealousy and place of pride. That is the humbling of pride in arrogance. No one will ever love your children more than you.

Do you know how a lion marks his territory? He pisses on everything. But the lionesses don't do that. Don't you find that interesting? Men follow the same genre, and so do women. Now that is the animal nature.

But the great eagle and some turtles and some lesser birds, they find a mate and they mate for life, that once they have found that one being — And here we know this about eagles because during the scourge of DDT[5] that those great and wonderful male and female eagles — who fed on lesser creatures that fed on fruits, vegetables, and wheatstuffs sprayed with DDT — that none of their eggs hatched, and so year after year they couldn't foster any young. Now did the male leave the female because he thought it was her fault that they didn't have babies? Never did. And today, today, this is the wisdom of the eagle, this is the wisdom of some turtles, this is the wisdom of some birds; not all, some. And we should take those "somes" and put them to

---

5 Chemical insecticide used for agriculture. It has been prohibited in the U.S. since 1973.

the highest point in their genetic order. These birds mate for life. If you kill the male bird, the female will never mate with another male, never. If you kill the female, the male, which everyone knows is propelled by his loins, that male will never mate again with another bird.

Now I want to ask you something: So as human beings do we find ourselves in the order of animals or do we find ourselves in the order of humans? And can we search in the animal kingdom and find true love, loyalty, and trust, or do we dispatch the animal part of us that all animals are the same way?

Even in the animal kingdom there is love. And the love that I am speaking about is a love that resonates in seven seals, and we are going to learn about that, that even the eagles know absolutely deep, passionate love; they know absolute trust, absolute dependency, and they know that their mate is irreplaceable. And how greater are you than eagles? I don't think very great. I don't think very great at all, because male eagles still loved female eagles when the shells of their young were so weak they couldn't bear young. So we have the classic syndrome of two beings incapable of producing living young, but they stay together. It is not uncommon to see a male eagle fly and be alone, and they are all loners. He does not run about. This is a nature being that has found completeness and in his completeness does not need or have even the urge to breed every early spring; he doesn't even have the urge to breed any longer.

Many of you have never been outside of your own living room or your own table of food, but if you ever ventured and observed nature, like I did and some of you in this audience have done, you will find out that the greatest of all the sexes in nature is the female, because rearing the young is upon her shoulders. That is the greatest of the sexes. I know you men don't like that, but let me tell you something: You name all of the creatures in nature that after copulation are left the responsibility of rearing the young. Now you will understand how powerful women are and how powerful the female gender is. There are exceptions. Female energy in any man is not to make himself a vagina. Female energy in a man is the strength to carry on with responsibility, which most men are not accustomed to doing. That is a truth.

So do migratory animals have love? Yes, they have sexual love. Now the purists amongst you will call that as humanistic or animalistic human behavior or animal behavior, as simply the season in which to propagate the species. But in fact when the hormones rage in any creature, including you, you will drop your drawers for anybody that says you are special. And to a doe with a big handsome buck, she is the queen of the day for about three days, and to the lioness, she is the queen for about ten days. To a bitch dog, she is the queen for as long as she is in heat. And ain't that just like your own life, that as long as you were in heat, it was on, it was special, you were unique, you were the only one. You — you, you, you; I am looking for the next word, you, you — you came together on many occasions, and then the temperature started to drop and it was a struggle after that. It is true. Men who wander around are animals. Women who are running around are looking for the big buck, the three-day, the four-day, the seven-day, the fourteen-day heat cycle. And then they are mad at their men because they are wandering around. Well, hell, they married an animal. They went to bed with an animal. What do you expect?

And then there are those great, special creatures. The reason I say this — Hey, I know you think that you are the greatest intelligence on the face of the Earth. No one understands you, not even a butterfly. Yeah, right. You see, I don't need to teach you these things. All you have to do is study nature and you will find out that there absolutely is love in the animal kingdom, and it is love of such a passionate order that — Imagine this: a great raptor. And this, by the way, happens to be one of two raptors that does this; most other raptors don't do this. But the great eagle is also — He is not and she is not simply a carnivorous animal; they are omnivorous, but no one ever sees them plucking berries and leaves to feed to their children.

So how do you explain a great male eagle watching his wife being shot or ending up in electrical lines and dying and he spends the rest of his life in solitary? They have something wonderful, something wonderful. It is called love. That pair that lost one another was so complete with that partnership that that partnership cannot be replaced. That is what all of you are looking for. You are looking for the perfect woman and the perfect man who in your life is irreplaceable.

CHAPTER 2
How Do You Make Love to a Woman?

A Blend of Indomitable Strength and Compassion

Tonight is dedicated simply to that which is termed the female gender in understanding, in all these years that we have been together, that men and women are only that which is termed the mechanical vehicle for a God that is neither.

So now what did you see in the light[1] before you came back here? You saw that which is termed a gender endeavoring to combine that which is termed compassion and love with strength. But strength has always been that which is termed the prerequisite to the man because the man was always that which went out and fought for the family's honor, which went out and fought the wild beasts of that which is termed the forest to bring home that which is termed foodstuffs. So the man actually always represented in every society the strength of the family union.

But if we take into consideration the strength that it takes of a woman from the fruit of the womb to usher forth in birth pains a new life, then we are talking about such pain that few men have ever, ever experienced. Now so when many entities say there are more women that are drawn to a new movement than men, there is truth in that because women have always possessed the side of strength, but unfortunately they have never been given that which is termed the permission to call it strength, because strength, as it were, to bring forth children into the world could

---

1 The light or life review after death.

43

never be measured in the masculine world. The masculine world only measures strength as to getting up every day and laboring into that which is termed the fields, to bring home the food to feed the family.

But the male never understood the female's worry, anxiousness, anxiety, and indomitable strength to bring forth children into the world. And they in one sense are closer to God because they know what it is to go inside and to expand themselves and to give of themselves that which is termed a new lifeform. Women were always considered the ultimate Goddess because they were the ones who ultimately on a matter-of-fact level turned inward and conceived and then brought outward that which is termed the fruit of the womb. How many of you understand? And so we understand that which is termed the understanding of nature, that nature is that which is termed a feminine gender because nature gives life and it takes away life. It is the woman who bears the responsibility of the new life. And of her body, her body is sapped of its vital life force to give that which is termed life to the new child that will come forth into a freed land.

So tonight we understand from the Observer's point of view the feminine. And from the feminine's point of view, as the Observer who gets to understand both parts of the polaric spectrum, we begin to see how the Observer set forth that which is termed not in the enjoyment of lust but the need of lust to reconcile that which is termed individual experience in a woman.

We see then that the power of the woman — fragile, much softer, much more "aqualine," much more beautiful than the features of a man — we saw that their bodies are soft. We saw that their bodies were able to that which is termed to produce and to carry a child, to receive the semen of a man, and to be able to enlarge itself to be able to support a child and then have that which is termed the downy softness of skin in which to cradle a new lifeform, as if we were being cradled in the bosom of God itself.

We see how the Observer then could choose in a life to be a woman, because in a woman we see softness, yet strength. We see beauty, yet sovereignty. We see that which is termed creativeness from the womb itself, that which is termed the Void re-creating itself.

So now why did man always fear woman? Because woman was never governed by the places that man in his first seal was, that woman was governed from a higher order naturally, and the higher order is survival. Whereas man, who cannot bear the heat of the forthcomingness of his seed, must have his way, a woman gives her way only because she sees that in the fortuitous sight of survival itself. And a woman will give herself not in passion but in survival. A woman's ultimate root of passion is not passion but survival, whereas man, the ultimate root of passion is passion. How many of you understand? So be it.

So if women work from a greater point in the seals, then that means that their power place has always been the third seal, that they could control pain and sexuality as that which is termed recommended to them to their survival. Men could never control their first seal in survival. They never could. It was always the undoing of every man. It was his Achilles' heel. A man who was weak in his first seal could always be conquered. I knew that in my lifetime. Don't you understand that we could send the greatest hetaera to that which is termed my greatest enemy and always find him weak, and the one enemy who wasn't weak to that was an enemy worthy of battle? Do you understand that? I knew that as a man.

Women, on the other hand, have a jump-start on evolution. Men are created to spill their seed every moment of the day that they are replenished. Women have only one cycle a month to which they are only that which is termed passion, and that passion is greatest when it is afforded their reproductive cycle. Any other time other than that, their passion is seduction, and their seduction is their power. How many of you understand?

I want you to pause for a moment and look at this. Look how many women I have around me. Even the most virile of you men and the most seductive of you men do not have this sort of audience. Well, my, my. I am only a personality in this woman's body. How do you account for this? What are they attracted to? Let me tell you a little secret, you old men of wise, sage belief: In my day all of these women would have gladly come to my tent. And even today I can love your women greater than you can. I can. I can. So what do I know that you do not know, my beloved fellow masters? What do I know you do not know? You look upon me and I am just a wee, little woman.

Now why? Because I considered them equal, I considered that they were God. And the closer they acted like that, the more beautiful they were to me, and that anytime you look upon the God[2] of a woman instead of her femininity — Her breasts, her vagina, her legs, her buttocks, her body, how much she weighs, how much she doesn't weigh, anytime that that becomes a standard of measurement to you, you have lost a very elevated entity. And they, of course, the elevated entity, doesn't know they are elevated because they have never been exposed to anything greater than what they can possibly get. Are you listening to me?

---

2 Ramtha's use of the word God must not be confused with any of the various religious traditions. It rather means our true self, our unique mind and free will, our real, indelible identity.

So how does a man make love to a woman? By loving her divinity above anything else — her face, her body, her breasts, her vagina, how she is in your bed — but to love that first and foremost because that speaks to the eternalness of her being because, after all, her isn't a her. Do you understand?

And most of you men in the audience, all you think about is how young a face is, how skinny the body is, how much breast there is, how much womb there is, how much, because you can only get one who is equal to your first seal. But it is yet now another challenge to have one who is equal to your third seal. And all women naturally are third-seal entities because in and of themselves they are not first-seal entities. They use the first seal as a place of power and only power. 'Tis a great truth.

So how indeed then must you start to change, my beloved men of this audience? And if any woman in this audience that is in the Great Work is worth her salt, she should never settle for one who will only placate her for the sake of her sexuality but will understand and communicate with her on the level of the divine and nothing but the divine, because when that is considered equal, everything else follows. To be less than that, if you ask a woman, "Love you this man," most of them will say yes. But if you have the vision to look at them, you will see that they tell you that because — they say that only because — it is for the children they have bore to this man, and that this man is not only the root of the survival of their children and/or the root of the survival of themselves, or they, as it were, will be the survivalist in the family so that the children can have their natural father.

Women, more than any other who are closest to the fourth seal, do not understand love because they have always had to anchor down, to love, to the first seal, the second seal, in order to make their way in life. And to have had a greater and a higher standard, their fears were always brought up about spinsterhood and ugliness and overweightedness. And all of the silly things that you try to become for the sake of men, you have anchored down already your evolutionary step for that which is termed an image ideal that in the end is going to give way to the worm itself.

What Is True Love Really About?

Is true love about appearance? Is true love about that which is termed youth or age, or is true love that which is termed something that cannot be calibrated in the first three seals but is calibrated only in the fourth? And if we say that women use their passion to control and to seduce willing men who are willing only to be serviced — this is an ugly term, to service a man, and many of you do that — you service them so that you can keep yourself in their space of focus, all along denying the power of the place that you sit; that if you were able to love from that place of power, and you were able to garner to yourself first the recognition that you are God, and that maybe you have been a man and that you have been many times a woman, so who is it that we must then reconcile ourself to?

We were born into this plane as polaric entities, negative to positive, that attraction that is so strong that it is no wonder that the energy of that attraction sits in the first seal, that it sits in the first seal for the sake of propagation. But in ten and a half million years you have evolved somewhat to understand that though this can be recreational, it is not time-honored commitment, and that indeed the greatest mates of our being we will never be attracted to here[3] — we will be attracted to here[4] because it is God to God. This will always feel righteous but it will not feel the heat of this[5] in the beginning. If this is the heat in the beginning, then it is doomed because it can only replicate itself so far as to be bored with itself, because as long as there is a restless Spirit in men and women, they will never be happy with their partner. And why? Because their partner never really represents who they really are. And until you begin to seek out that which you really are, are you going to be filled in all the seals to which is the level of your own evolution.

What Does It Mean to Be a Woman?

Now tonight I want you to know that these women's emotional bodies are set and geared biologically and genetically, which we are talking about the DNA or gender here. They are geared for that which is termed survival, and children have always been a part of their survival, and if it has not been children, it has been the pleasure of sexuality. But most women have their greatest comfort sexually when they know that they have owned their man. I want you to understand it is a truth. And though they may gain pleasure from it, they work and labor specifically in which to become everything so sexually that they who labor so much, if you say to them, "Why do you work so hard on being beautiful; why do you work so hard on being thin; why do you work so hard on being a hetaera; why?" and the answer is "to keep my

---

3 The first seal, sexual attraction.
4 The fourth seal, unconditional love.
5 Sexual urgency of the first seal.

man happy," an enlightened being would look at that and say if you have to live your life for the momentary pleasure of a man, you are already dead. You are already dead. If you are having to live to capture a certain individual, that means you are dying to your enlightenment for the sake of the comfort of a person who is not equal to you. The day that women recognize that their equality is in God and not in men is the day they get to share the journey of men, who also see that their equality is in God and not in women, on the journey back home. So be it.

And if you have to gear down to someone and you have to deny to someone and you have to pretend to be something other than what you really are, that is not evolutionary. You are going to die, and you will be born again in this body with the same curse every twenty-one days until you realize what you are really here to be.

Now what does it mean to be a woman? It means that God is closer to being realized, because the womb of creation sits right below the fourth seal and that in realization we must make a decision: Are we going to then live our life as women, prone to our moods and indeed our bodies, are we going to live our life prone to the necessity of having someone make us feel great, or do we live our life first and foremost that we are God in a woman's body and delight in being the woman, delight in being beautiful, delight in being old, delight in having wisdom, delight in our bodies, and in that we are virtuous because then we are real? When we do that, then we are nearer to God. And we say then that this will eliminate 99.9 percent of the world's men from our life, then so be it. "I can walk this life alone and become nearer to my God." That is the way it is. Or to that which is termed a wonderful happiness, we find an opposite gender, a man, who has thought the same, who shares our life, and to eliminate them because of our prejudice is as much a backward manifestation as the one that we have struggled to come up from.

Now I have men and women here who are really Gods, the forgotten Gods. This body is a garment. Its emotions controlled you; that is why you came to school. You are here not to be better men and women but to finally be God, the most important thing. That is what a master is all about. A master has to be beautiful to no one but God. And it is not what we look like but how we are morally: our thoughts, our Observer. If our Observer can see the fallacy of our humanity, the day our Observer sees itself is the day we have arrived at godhood. In other words, the day that our Observer sees life without the positive or the negative is the day that our God has become ourself. That is the beginning of our Christhood.

Women cannot live their life for the sake of being a woman. And the day that their common thought becomes that of God instead of their feminine gender — in other words, the day that the Observer observes the Observer — is the day that we have immortal life. For women that is closer than for men. That is the reason why there are so many crossovers in the world, so many men in prior lives that have become women, because a woman is the path that is closest to redemption. 'Tis a truth.

And men have the longest, hardest journey of the two because their whole image is connected to their penis. Every part of their physical maturity is connected to their penis. Men have a hard time every day getting up and going through the day without ejaculation. Women don't have a problem. The day that the man no longer is connected to his penis but is connected to his fourth seal and works arduously to be that and can still consider himself a God, not a man, is the day that he is nearer to God and he is on the equal precipice with women.

Sexual Revolution and Freedom

Now there has certainly been in the twentieth century a revolution for women's liberation. And women's liberation gave them the permission to have multiple lovers and not feel guilty about it, and gave them the permission to have passion without the responsibility of children. And this then was dreamed into reality: for you to love many men and have no children, as you wished; to know what it was to be a man in previous lifetimes who had that ability to do that, a man who can love a woman and walk away from the fruit of her womb and from her. You have gotten in this century the opportunity to do that. That is not by accident; that was created. So with birth control came, as it were, your liberation to a greater point of degree to where you got to live your passionate life and explore it without responsibility. That is not a bad thing. That is an evolutionary evolvement.

Now most of you who got to see that have come to the shallow point that, as you were on an equal standard of men and women, got to understand that there is an emptiness and hollowness about that which is termed sexuality. And if you did, it is those of you who came to this school who said I have had the liberation to be all of these things but I am garnered to yet a higher degree of understanding. That higher degree of understanding says that I obviously chose this life and I obviously had the ability to choose this life to exercise my discretion in childbearing. Perhaps in this life I had the ability and I earned the ability to explore those forbidden areas, that — save for only hetaerae, who knew the science of cycles in women, did not have to have children — I can finally learn and explore those regions. Now that I have explored them, I have found that which is termed it is empty to lie with a man who loves me only for my body and is yet concerned not for my deeper thoughts, and yet it is my deeper thoughts that govern me and guide me throughout this life.

You got through your emotional body the freedom of sexual freedom without responsibility. When do you say then I know what that is; I know what it is to lie with a man without the responsibility of the man and indeed without the responsibility of his children? When do you have enough that you can say when is it then I can lie with God and have the responsibility of God? When then can I finally see this is so empty and here I am in the place that I have geared down forever and ever and ever from my place of power? Can I use power — which is will, manipulation, cleverness, stalwartness, frankness — can I use that same asset to catapult myself into a greater realm? And indeed am I willing to leave behind the world's men who are brought up in the nursery of the world, and can I leave it behind and perhaps on my way find a companion or find not a companion? That is what the mastery of women is all about.

Women need to understand that they are not less than men, and that they should never be property of men, and indeed that they should not feel that the only thing that is good about them is their uterus or their bosom or their buttocks, and that to think that is not to love yourself. I want you to know that. If you are endeavoring to live for the affections of a man by the way you look, then you are already dead and have never wakened up, because men traditionally live from their first seal.

But men's greatest competition is not women but it is men on the third seal in what is called competition. Men love to beat men at their own games — women are passive — in that which is termed only to have relief from the sperm that is built up in their loins. I want you to know that. And men take women so as to offer that which is termed an indignancy to their fellow man to say, "I got this woman and now you don't have them." It is the harem concept. Harem concept in mentality in men is old. It is old.

The day that my women say, "I am living for my God, and I will live from that morality, and indeed I will live from that beauty, and I will live from that clarity, and I will not sell my body short for any man who enters my sphere for the sake of making him feel grand, I will keep myself for my God," is a wise woman and a wise woman who will never sell herself short ever again to belong to a harem, because men are fickle. Men are fickle. When they live in their first seal, they can never be truthful. If they live in their fourth seal, they are honored by the stamp of God. It is this that you want and nothing else. You should no longer be less than what you have naturally always been.

And this speaks to all of the men in the audience, as well, who feel the same way. You should never feel that you need to leave that which is termed a higher order to play the game of a lower order. You don't need to do that. If you are not living your life for what society thinks about you, then it is time that you dispense with the fallacies of your life and start living a truism, start living righteously. Who cares what the world thinks? Who cares who you are with? Who cares if you are alone? Who cares what the men in your circle say? If you are on the path, that is all that matters to your God. Who cares what say they? And perhaps then that is your challenge and indeed that is your mastery.

I honor the women tonight because forever they have been herded like cattle into harems. They have been bought and sold. They have been taken into marriage only to be betrayed. The men who gave them their honor they would be true to them always lied, and it was understood that they could lie. But the women were never allowed to be anything other than their word.

I want my women in this audience who smoke pipes with me to understand they are liberated, and they are liberated not in a sexual liberation but in their God liberation, that they have lived ten and a half million years of life. Who haven't you been? What haven't you been in ten and a half million years? If you haven't been better than you think your dreams are, you have been uncreative in your past ten and a half million years.

Greatness, real greatness, that epic of memory: Who in this audience do you think is going to be remembered two thousand years from tonight? Do you think the most beautiful woman in this audience is going to be remembered two thousand years from now? They won't. Do you think the ugliest man in this audience is going to be remembered two thousand years from now? How about the most beautiful man in this audience; do you think he is going to be remembered two thousand years from now? Sorry, you don't register.

What is remembered? An entity who lives their truth, be it male or female — and females rarely. It is time that you become torches in the new millennium. It is true. I tell you your God in you is not prejudiced as gender is prejudiced. Your God chose you for a reason. You bring to the table of evolution opportunity, not sexuality. Remember that. Your God chose this body for opportunity and not sexuality. And if you do not create opportunity, master it, and are willing to own it as wisdom, then you will only go down in the graveyards of the West or the East as something that was remembered and smells badly. Do you understand?

Is Sex a Wrong Thing?

So now we gathered together and we began to see how it is no wonder why there are more women who vacillate to the truth, because it is closer to them; it is what they really are. And whenever women can really apply the message, without going down and take it up, are the ones that go home very easily.

So, my beautiful women, is sexuality a wrong thing? No, it is not. But it becomes a disgrace to your honor as a God when you abuse it for the sake of survival; then it dishonors you. And you should never keep company with that which dishonors you — ever, ever. You are born nearer to God. From nearer to God you should go upward with it. And, yes, it is a very powerful test, especially when you are young or when you are about to lose that which is termed the blush of your maidenhood. Then you are panicked because what will the world think of you as that which is termed wrinkles and sags and all of that starts in on your body; what will they think of you?

But you have to ask yourself who are you pursuing. Are you pursuing the youth of ignorance? Are you pursuing the wisdom of eternity? Young people don't know any better. Do you really want to give up your life for the sake of an inexperienced and ignorant person? A wise man or a wise woman would never do that. And do you want to panic that you are losing your youth? Now there is reason to panic because you have lived by your body's emotion for so long. What will happen when you look in the mirror and it is no longer beautiful when it looks back at you? What are you going to do?

But who are you being beautiful for, yourself or what the world thinks? If you live for what the world thinks, you are already dead. You will never hear anything else I have to say to you. But if you look at your beautiful self and cultivate all of the wisdom that you have learned, and if you can peel the onion, peel it until you find the core — why did I do this, I did it for this; why did I do that, I did it for that; and why did I do this, I did it for that — and if you can find the core of all of your reaction, you have found truth, and it will set you free.

How many times have you been women in the course of ten and a half million years? I would say more than fifty percent. How many times have you been young and beautiful? More than fifty percent. How many more times can you be that? More than fifty percent. When is the day that you take a chance and say, "Can I cultivate something other than physical wisdom — how about my mind? — and not settle for anything other than that which matches my mind?" The day that you do that is the day that you are awakened and nearer to God. The day you don't do that is when you are nearer to your femininity.

Women are awesome beings. Don't you know that the whole strategy of men for all of this time to enslave you and to mark you and to cattle you and to use you and abuse you is because you had a power because you were a law unto your own self? Don't you know that there was something to be afraid of there and to use? If you weren't anything that was threatening, you would never have been herded like cattle, never would have been, nor would have religion set out to permanently destroy who you are.

This business about Mary having children when she is a virgin, obviously a man of myth created that. You learn to be your own person and don't you ever trade your body for security. Don't you ever do that. Don't you ever do that. You have done that many lifetimes. Don't you ever do that again. And don't you ever take someone to your bed that is less than you. Don't you ever do that. And you go about creating your enlightenment for the sake of you. Don't you know you are worthy to fall in love with? And don't you know that the long, dry spell of walking the path, that sooner or later some beautiful entity is going to join you who is also there?

Rare are masters. The reason that they are not rare is because of their sexuality. But that is why this is called the plane of demonstration. So is there that fear that as you have grown older you wasted your youth on a cattleman's idea or indeed that which is termed an idea that you threw away your youth and your volatility? You only have to have intercourse one time to understand what it is. After the hymen is broken, we should have wisdom.

Look, every event I watch you and I watch the games you play. You think that I miss anything? I don't miss anything. I know who is playing a game to get this person interested in them and that person interested in them. I know what you are doing. Don't you know? Of course you know. But did you ever stop and think that there was a knowingness that knew you were doing that? What about going after that knowingness? What can it offer you? Everything that you don't see in front of you.

You are just fine without a man in your life. You are just fine. You really are. You are just as important and you are just as beautiful and you are natural. You are actually supernatural. You are just as important without your breasts and your vagina and your face because — think about this — the face and the breasts and the vagina become only a small part of life. Think about birth to death and what part of that are you really beautiful. How many years are you fertile and beautiful before you start to age? It is less than a third. What are you going to do with the rest of it? Are you going to live in regret and anger and unhappiness?

What you have to do is start now and say, "I am enough. I have always been enough," and you have to live for your ideal. You have to live for what gives you comfort and what gives you beauty and what gives you truth. You cannot rely on any man for truth. You have to rely on yourself. Furthermore, you cannot rely on any man to support you. You need to support yourself because to do anything otherwise is to have affairs and liaisons for the sake of survival and not for meaningful existence. How many of you understand? So be it.

The Focus Should Be What Are You As a Mind

Now, my beloved people, have you learned tonight? We understood that that which is termed emotion and chemicals are the voices in your head. You also learned that that which talks to you up here has an ulterior motive, and the ulterior motive is emotion. It is only chemicals that talk to the neuronet. That is why it sounds like a voice.

So most of you respond to the voices in your head because indeed you are responding to chemical emotion. Chemical emotion is a past; present has yet to be felt. We want to create a future-present; we create that which is termed a future that starts off with an ideal. The ideal, we should know, is not going to have any emotion, and the only thing we are going to feel, if feeling can be interpreted as the proper term, is the freedom to be able to create this concept. The concept is not going to feel like anything. You are addicted to feeling.

59

New concepts don't feel any of these things. If anything, they feel like they are free. That is the path of the master.

Now listen to me, particularly my women. You are emotional beings because you have always gone backwards in order to refacilitate an emotion and consequently you have never grown in your life. You have always held to your bed that which was equal to a past, never what you really dreamed about being. When we create from the Observer, we should know whatever we create is not going to have an emotion with it. Women's tendency is to rush and find an emotion. I don't want you to do that. You know why I tell you it is your tendency to do that? Because your whole survival with men for a very long time genetically has been to find what makes them feel good. Men love it when you make them feel good, but they don't like it when you are not making them feel good. And you have learned that.

So one of your great strategies is to create an emotional situation that the man can solve because that is who you go to with your emotional problems. But didn't you ever really listen, if you think about it, to the voice in your head that already knew the answer? You were playing a game, and you have always played games. The truth is you already knew the answer and you were putting on this play, and you have even watched yourself do it. You have watched yourself create unnecessary problems for solving by the other gender. That said it all. That has to be dispensed of, and it has to be dispensed of because you have got to stop being clever; you have got to start being real. You can always go down to the nearest welfare office to get food. You don't have to prostitute your intelligence for the sake of somebody giving you a meal, which you have always done. And you don't have to prostitute yourself to make the man feel better.

You may come to this wonderful realization that when you really become real — real — and just are who you are without playing any game, yes, you are going to have to maybe lose the person who is sharing your bed, but maybe the next person who shares your bed will be your equal. You understand?

And are there equals? Absolutely. Are there equals for men? Absolutely, because just as I am telling you this, there are men in this audience who already know the program. And they sell themselves out sexually because they understand the whole game. And they play the game because they are satisfied sexually and they can be supported. Do you understand?

See, what we want to do is to get rid of the whole onion of the polarity itself and just become beings — not male or female; beings — that we share an equal footing with one another. And we can only have in our life what is equal to our God intelligence; not our gender intelligence, our God intelligence. How many of you understand that?

And you women, you are the cleverest of them all. You know why? Because your energy sits in the third seal. And man's most vulnerable place is his penis, and you know that. You do. The day that you stop going down and gearing down and start gearing up is the day we go home to God. Easy.

And men, the day that they stop living in their penis, in their image, and can at least move to the place of sovereign power — to be able to leave behind their past and know that it is their past — is the day they sit on the same precipice, is the day that they can move into the fourth seal and the fifth seal. But no man ever moves into these kingdoms until he has owned his power and indeed owned that which he thinks he is in terms of his penis and his image. If we were to make every man in this audience a eunuch, who would he be without his manhood? Would he still be able to share the bed with his lover? Would he still be able to share communication? Would he still be able to do that? If he did that, if he were able to do that, then that is a sure sign that he is not his sexuality. And he should never want to be loved but for anything but his true self, of which he himself every day is defining.

New frontiers of self are never-ending. The past of who we are is already known, and it is boring. There is no man in this audience who is more gifted than another man. It is just the way it is. And if they are braggarts, they are fools. I know how men are. Any man who brags about his sexuality is just looking for a harem. You understand? The noble man never does that, and the noble man does not use his sense of sexuality in which to own a woman. Any true man in this audience that is nearer to God will think himself less a man and more God. You understand? The same with you women.

Now what is your morality when it comes to the teaching of what a master is and what a master isn't? So what is a master? A master is one that does not use their body, their face, their breasts, their uterus, their wealth — trying to be skinny, trying to be fat; it doesn't matter — tries not to use that to diminish what they really are. The focus should be what are you as a mind. Mind doesn't really possess gender; did you know that? We don't have in classical science the female mind or the male mind; we only have mind. I say to you it is better to strive to be a mind and have the image of a mind rather than a body, for if you do, then you will join the great and illustrious ranks of masters.

If you always think in terms of competition, if you think in terms of how skinny you are — how many times you miss meals so that you will look the way that you do, how many times you eat so as to pacify what is not given to you — if every time your focus is on your body instead of your mind, you lose. This audience is about being a master. So what is a woman master? One that does not use her body to get what she wants; second, that does not play upon the tragedy of her past to get what she wants; and, third, one who can be who she is from two minutes ago.

Any one of you, and many of you up here, sit and bark and complain about what happened to you in your past. What would you be if you didn't have that memory? Could you stand on your own? Could you? Could you be as beautiful, enthralling, as intriguing, as mindful, if you didn't have to snare a man because of all the terrible things that happened to you? Listen, terrible things happen to everybody. You are not unique. No one here is unique. So would you be able to be as beautiful without a past as you are with one? And if you can eliminate the past and simply be who you are and stand on the merits of your wisdom, then that is something to be proud of. If you can't, you have nothing to be proud of; you are already dead. And any great man who is a master already knows that. You understand?

You cannot entice a master with your victimization. You cannot entice a master with your beauty, with your body. You cannot do that. You only entice a master when you can share equal mind. The morality of women is: Do not use your body to get where you think you are going, and do not use your past to make up where you think your body lacks. Do not control and manipulate someone if you are not in control of yourself — got that? — and to love yourself above all else. And if no one else in this world loves your eyes, loves your face, loves your body, no matter how much you have eaten, no one else loves it but you, that is enough. And anyone after that is more than your fair share. You understand? And then you will be happy. Then you are the rarest amongst jewels.

Most women are never happy until they have got someone in their bed. If you can be happy without any man or woman and simply happy with yourself, you are a jewel beyond price. I would rather be nearer to God than nearer to a man or a woman's heart. So it is said by Christ, "Seek ye first the kingdom of heaven and everything else will be given after you." That is a truth, and to do anything otherwise is to compromise; you are already dead.

Love your children with all your might and with all your heart, and give with them every moment you feel that you were never given to. Languor with them, love with them, and teach them righteously. And never, ever let your children see you insecure, and never, ever show yourself insecure. You take care of that before you ever walk nobly in front of your children. And you teach them how to rectify all problems, and you teach them not prejudice; you teach them love and strength. You teach them that beauty is not everything but nobility and courage are everything. You teach them that who they are must be developed, and that when they are developed to the point of their own acceptance, only then — only then — do they find themselves acceptable to the world and not anytime sooner or later.

You have to teach them that they are good enough and it is they who are here on this journey. You are their mothers. You teach them that. You teach them love and you teach them forgiveness and you teach them righteousness. You do not teach them anything other than that. You do not teach them lies. You do not teach your daughters how to manipulate. You do not teach your daughters to grow up early. You do not teach your sons to grow up early. You teach them to be children, to learn to explore, to learn to love, to learn to understand, to wallow in the innocence of children. And when they come into their adulthood, you teach them responsibility of their bodies but always from the point of view that they are in control — you got that? — and to give them up for the folly of a man is a foolish thing.

It is your hour to be the great teacher. It is your hour to love unconditionally. It is your hour to teach and to love. Never give up your children for any man. Do you hear me? Never. So be it. And I don't care if no one else in the world thinks you are beautiful. I do, and your God does. Don't live for the flesh; live for the mind. And the mind will reward you a millionfold.

Your Highest Compliment — Your Mind, Not Your Body

Now are you listening? So what in the world does this teaching have to do with the Observer?[6] Everything, because the Observer is impartial. You should know that. The Observer is impartial. And the Observer in how we observe something is impartial to how we will feel it. Are you with me?

Most men and women have always been segregated — and, of course, here we are with a segregated group of women and spattered with a few men — to explain that which is termed the war of the sexes. There isn't any war because basically up until this point everyone has lived by their emotions, their instincts, their bodily feelings. Look, you are in the school of the Great Work. If you were out there on the street tonight he'ing and she'ing, you wouldn't even listen to what I am having to say, though you would wish Monday morning you

---

6 See Fig. F: The Observer Effect and the Nerve Cell, and Fig. G: Cellular Biology and the Thought Connection, pp. 252-253.

would have had a few words of wisdom. But tonight, no. You are here to learn.

The Observer in women is no different than the Observer in men. It is just women process the Observer differently than men do. The difference is men process it usually and unlayer it all the way to their first seal and women do it to their third seal. That is the difference. And in a world where everything is based on the first three seals, then it is women who have to grapple with that which is termed security. Men grapple with success. Men are not afraid to fail in front of women but they are terrified to fail in front of other men.

So women are the true amazons. They are the real warriors. They know what it is to go out and make war and save family and hearth. They do. That is why their power has been subjugated for eons, because they are a law unto themselves. So what does this have to do with the teaching? And it is simply this: that the Observer in women's greatest caution they have to watch out for is their power over men. And if women would take the power and take it on up instead of down, they would go to their seventh seal easily — easily.

Men with the Observer have a much more difficult time because their feelings on anything and everything they create has to do with success, and the success is always anchored in sexuality. Are you listening to me? They have a very hard road. And that hard road is that you can take an enlightened man and put him with a hetaera, and he will drink the waters of forgetfulness nearly all of his life. He will be enslaved by the tiger, and that is when the women always win. I don't care what you say. They always have, except that unfortunately they have never been given the power to lead; they have always done it through their sexuality or through their sons.

Now in going to become a master, there are men and

women masters and they are considered equals; they are not considered unequals. And they have their respective beauty. Men who are masters are beautiful, beautiful, according to the decree of their beauty. Women are breathtaking. They are beautiful according to the decree of their law. But in masters, there is an equalness; there is not an unequalness. There is a sharing. We do not have masters in this realm that live in the first seal and then the others in the fourth seal. They are not masters. They are all on equal bearing. They can only exist in a dominion to where everyone is equal.

So how do women reconcile finally being given equality? Can they still be beautiful and can they still be feminine and still they can be elegant and still be powerful? Yes, there are many who do. Are there women who then, because their beauty has been such a degradation to them, find themselves marred and ugly and that is the way they reach their masterhood? Yes, but don't you know we all understand that. It is called the journey.

And are there men who are virile and beautiful and look like the Gods or the sun God himself? Yes. And are there men who are masters who are ugly and scarred and torn? Yes, because whatever took us there and whatever we cherish is what we get to be, because when we arrive, it has nothing to do with the way we look. It is what we are, the substance of what we are.

Look, I chose a woman's body because they were the most prejudiced group that have ever lived and yet they are the most powerful group; otherwise there would never have been the conspiracy in religion to subvert them. Don't you think I know a sword when I see a sword? And liberating them has been tantamount. Every great prophet that has ever shown its face has been the face of a man, which has left women little to worship and idolize, except maybe nature and herbs and flowers and food and the hearth and their sons. Don't you understand that? Very few women are ever proud of their daughters because in survival they understand the journey. They just do. It is a hard-fought wisdom. I chose a woman because every time I come out here and speak to you, that is the beautiful face you look upon. And can a beautiful face know so much and be so even and be unattached? Can a beautiful face really be God and not be persuaded? Yes. And can it hold power? Absolutely.

Mary, mother of Yeshua ben Joseph, is such a pitiful archetype. No wonder she cries all the time. I want all of you to know that what you can become is like me. You do not have to be a man. You don't have to be a man. All you have to do is be yourself and have your substance, your morals, and your standards be unimpeachable. Then you will be like me.

You can still be as beautiful as you want to be, as ugly as you want to be. You can be as old as you want to be; you can be as young as you want to be. It is all on your terms. The most important thing that you love about me is me, and I cannot be seen. Don't you see? All those times in front of the mirror, and all those foods that you refused to eat, all those things that you overeat, don't you understand this had nothing to do with substance? It is this, and it comes out of the eyes and it is beautiful.

You are that close. Don't use your sexuality to find another husband. Use your God to find yourself. Is that to say then that you are going to be abstinent all through your journey? Maybe. It doesn't really matter if you are already fulfilled. We only need people because we have a lack in ourself. When we are totally fulfilled in ourself, everyone else is company. Do you understand? That is the most desirable woman on the face of the earth. That is the most desirable woman on the face of the earth, one who doesn't need anybody. Do you understand me?

You have always anchored downward and you have used your past — the abuses of your past, your culture, your religion, your parents — to hook into someone. And did you know all the time there was a part of you that knew you were doing that? You know that. And you marveled at your cleverness, but you were embarrassed and hated it at the same time because you really felt the things you felt, but yet your head was telling you something else. So who should you listen to, your heart or your head? Your head. And you used that. So you went down and you used your victim to the most, and then when you were ready, you laid the trap of your sexuality. And then to keep them there, you vacillated back to your victim. Are we talking truth here? Oh, yes, we are. And the most beautiful hetaera in here is going to get ugly and old.

So what if you just realized that what you already know here, that is laughing at what you are doing, why don't you follow its advice and go up? What have you got to lose for the next five years? Nothing. What if indeed you just became that which laughs at everything that you do? Why don't you just be that? Don't you know that the Gods from the Seven Sisters[7] will find you because you are not ordinary? And don't you know you will love yourself even more? And don't you know then you can't get rid of these flies because you are so sticky then? Don't you understand that is the way it works? Truth is freedom and it is also seductive. It is the highest compliment we pay ourself. Our body is not our highest compliment; our mind is.

I want you to be great women, all the way to great Gods. I don't want you to be afraid of anything. I don't want you to be afraid of time or your face or wrinkles or fat. I don't want you

---

7 The Pleiades.

69

to be afraid of food. I don't want you to be afraid of poverty. You don't be afraid of any of those because the Observer, that laughs when you are putting this dream together, is the same one that can make you rich, beautiful, and forever young. You got that? So be it.

It is just you have got to be brave enough to strike out on your own. And when you say march and no one else marches with you, you have to go. And if no one is there, stir up your own dust field. Got that?

Now I daresay if we do a personal reading on all of you, you have been women multitudinous times more beautiful than you are now, uglier than you are now, richer than you are now, poorer than you are now, courtesans, lepers. So what do you have to lose if it doesn't work? Why, you are going to be wiser when you go to the light, and you are just going to create a prettier body because that is all the substance you have gained from it. You understand? How many of you understand? So be it.

So now it is no kidding when I told you that the greatest army that ever existed in small part were women. They were the most vicious warriors there ever were. I could hack heads and have no grief. They could do it better than I could because their wrath was unforgivable. That is only to say where they really were and the kind of will that sits underneath their façade, their hypocrisy, their diplomacy.

When you just develop who you are, you will be more beautiful than you ever were before, and you can't be bought, and you can't be flattered, and you can't be sold. You understand? So be it. Then I promise you if you do as I tell you to do, in less than a fortnight you will see the virtue of the teaching. Not only will you no longer be sick in your bodies, because you don't have to keep resorting to your victimization, because it won't be there. So if it is not there, then we don't have those peptides going down to those cells and causing craziness. We don't have disease. And if we have honesty, we don't have to worry about time. So all you have to do is be the core of what you really are, that Observer. And that Observer then will give you immortal life, and you will never die of cancer or any other disease. Women have the greatest cancer associated with their gender because they play these games, and they hate themselves because in the back of their brain someone is laughing the whole time. You got that?

In a fortnight, if you just say the following things:

Let me live what is the voice in my mind.
Let me be it truthfully every moment.
Let me live not on another man's wealth
but on my own mind.
God manifest my mind to wealth, security, truthfulness,
and enrich my life
that I am a light in the field of the dead.
So be it.

That is all. Turn to your neighbor and tell them what you have learned.

INTERLUDE
The Perfect Lover

Let us pause here for a moment. The journey that awaits us right ahead is filled with mystery, the stories and secrets reserved for the table of masters, beings who have lived and seen it all and survived to tell us about it. Let me explain.

What is the secret for finding the perfect lover, the perfect love in our life that will never fade or turn ugly? The next three chapters approach this question from various angles, offering us a number of analogies, from bizarre medical conditions to popular stories to the ancient wisdom of masters offering us important clues.

Ramtha's sharp mind invites us to investigate: When we fall in love, what is the object of our attraction? When we say we love someone, what is it that inspires our dreams and imagination? What is it exactly that captures our attention and robs us of our waking thoughts? These are important questions, for not everybody agrees as to what love really is.

Love and beauty seem to belong to the same category, yet both pretty much depend on the eye of the beholder. The great Scottish philosopher and writer of the eighteenth century, David Hume, pointed out, "Beauty is no quality in things themselves: It exists merely in the mind which contemplates them; and each mind perceives a different beauty. One person may even perceive deformity, where another is sensible of beauty; and every individual ought to acquiesce in his own sentiment, without pretending to regulate those of others."[1] This is to say that the beauty we perceive and fall in love with is largely subjective, an affair of the mind that is not solely based on external characteristics, special attributes, or ratios and proportions of mathematical precision.

Ramtha's answer to this riddle is quite ingenious and unexpected. He shows that the secret of looking into someone's eyes holds a piece of the puzzle. The gaze of lovers into each other's eyes is hypnotic and mind-capturing, for in it the true identity of the person is what is being recognized, something beyond mere body parts, gender, or status in life. People who put all their efforts solely into physical beauty and the presentation of their bodies are reducing and limiting their identity to their physical body alone, setting themselves up for a love that cannot transcend beyond mere sexual love, sensual attraction. Their intimate thoughts, concerns, and ideals — their mind — are often left out of the picture, preparing the way for impending disaster, a fulfillment that is short-lived and that never reaches a significant level of intimacy and understanding.

The point being made is that love changes tone and color depending on how we see and define ourselves. If we see ourselves solely in terms of our physical body, then that is all we can expect to experience in terms of love. It will be a physical love and nothing else. No complaints about that. Infidelity should not be a concern here since the objective is sensual pleasure, however disguised or heavy-laden with guilt and responsibility it may be. This is not a matter of morality; it is simply a choice we

---

1 David Hume, *Essays Moral, Political, and Literary,* edited by Eugene F. Miller, revised ed. (Indianapolis, Indiana: Liberty Fund, Inc., 1987), *Essay XXIII, Of the Standard of Taste,* p. 230.

often make. "Love is a many-splendored thing," but in today's society, Ramtha explains with tremendous honesty, many people only get to experience "a trap of many-splendored ways."[2] The gifts of sensuality are used to catch people's attention not only in the areas of marketing and entertainment by big corporations but are also used individually to build new relationships that are supposed to be lasting and enriching.

Ramtha insists that the key lies in the mind, that "what makes love magical is not the act but the sacred that leads to the act, because it is all mind."[3] He explains that "true beauty is not to do with one's body. It is the originality of the Spirit, the dancing eyes and the mind that is quick, a Spirit that knows and understands challenges in life."[4]

Medical disorders of the mind such as amnesia and split personality call into question the true identity of a person. A person suffering amnesia can forget another person, including lovers and children, overnight. Amnesiacs still remember how to speak, walk, and function normally, yet they do not remember the past, the emotions they shared in common with those they loved. Their identity is altered drastically with this condition. Split Personality Disorder is another baffling condition that shows how our identities are deeply ingrained in the mind. The whole biorhythms of the body change in the twinkling of an eye the moment a split personality switches identities. Even complex ailments may totally disappear and reappear while switching from one personality identity to the next. This is not fantasy but a proven medical fact. Ramtha uses these examples from medicine

2 *Love Is a Many-Splendored Thing: Mastery and the Relationship Factor, Part I,* Tape 382.5. (Yelm: Ramtha Dialogues, 1998).

3 *Miracles Exist Outside Emotional Time,* Tape 422 ed. (Yelm: Ramtha Dialogues, 1999).

4 *Love Is a Many-Splendored Thing,* Tape 382.5.

to show that who and what we are is far more than merely our physical bodies.

One of the most exciting parts of this book is the story of Don Juan and Saint-Germain at the countess' house. This true story offers a perfect illustration of what lies at the heart of our deepest longing. In Ramtha's story the fictitious Spanish character Don Juan[5] — the prototype of the greatest lover — is in this case none other than Giacomo Casanova, Chevalier de Seingalt. Casanova was a notorious Venetian writer from the eighteenth century who mixed with the nobility of Europe, famous for seducing a great many of their women. The famous translator and editor of Casanova's original autobiography, Willard R. Trask, makes the comment in his introduction that "Giacomo became a good scholar, he attended the University [of Padua] (1738-1741), graduated, and later received minor orders. But to a career in the Church he eventually proved recalcitrant. For while [Antonio] Gozzi was trying to lead him toward it, the priest's younger sister Bettina was teaching him his real bent. In this his first love affair, it was the girl who was the seducer. After that one apprenticeship, he took the role himself. From then on the stages of his life are punctuated by women."[6]

---

5 The earliest mention of the character Don Juan in literature is in *The Trickster of Seville* by Tirso de Molina (1630). He appears in W. A. Mozart's opera *Don Giovanni* (1787). Ironically Casanova, together with Da Ponte, was involved in writing the opera's libretto for Mozart. The character reappears from time to time in various plays by Molière (1665), José Zorrilla (1844), in Lord Byron's famous poem, *Don Juan* (1819-1824), and in George B. Shaw's play, *Man and Superman* (1905).

6 Giacomo Casanova, Chevalier de Seingalt, *History of My Life*, translated by Willard R. Trask, Vol. 1 (New York: Harcourt, Brace & World, Inc., 1966), p.5.

Two unusual masters find each other at the same table: Saint-Germain, the great alchemist famous in the court of France for his fabulous wealth in diamonds and jewels, and Casanova, the greatest lover of his time.

In this story, Don Juan's greatest attribute was surely not his flawless physique, as we can all verify for ourselves by the various portraits of Giacomo Casanova available: "It was that he could look into a woman's eyes and converse with them and never look away, and never be impatient, and hold the moment. He knew how to make every person in his sight the only person in the world." Ramtha continues to explain, "That is why he was Don Juan, because all he had to do was look into those eyes and hold that gaze and he knew the soul of the person, and from that, intimacy flowered. It was beautiful." The secret of his success, adds Ramtha, was that "he seduced the intimacy of a person, not their body."[7]

Saint-Germain was famous for his fabulous wealth, his profound knowledge of exotic sciences, and his wisdom. Rumor had it that he had discovered the elixir of immortality and the alchemical secret for transmuting metals into gold, and could even make precious gems larger than their original size. In fact actual historical references to this unconventional master are extremely scarce. Casanova's own description of Saint-Germain in his famous autobiography is rather interesting:

"This very strange man, who was born to be the most arrant of impostors, would say, without being challenged and as if in passing, that he was three hundred years old, that he possessed the universal medicine, that he could do whatever he pleased with nature, that he melted diamonds and out of ten or twelve small ones made a big one no less

---

7 *Miracles Exist Outside Emotional Time,* Tape 422 ed.

in weight and of the finest water. These things were trifles for him."[8]

As we can clearly see, both Saint-Germain and Casanova were quite marvelous in their own right. One is a master of the occult knowledge of alchemy and the other is a master in the art of making love.

Ramtha throws in a challenging question: "And so who are they going to listen to, the greatest lover of their age or immortality?" This is to say, what is a greater mystery to the human mind, irresistible seduction or the desire for immortality and perpetual youth?

The ability to dream of such fantastic dreams as immortality and perpetual youth opens the stage for a greater, more expansive definition of who we can become and what caliber of experience we can hope for. The intensity and height of love's experience in the light of such reflection escapes what we can describe in words, for it is an experience we have yet to grasp and make our own.

This is what lies ahead in our journey once "we have seen it all and done it all"[9] and are ready for a greater life, a greater reflection of who we are. Then we will realize why the ancient wisdom of the ages insists time and time again that "to love another person means the unequivocal love of yourself,"[10] that in order to find the perfect lover in our life, we must find love first in ourselves — our reflection in the mirror — everything we see and know about us. After all, did not the masters also say that the whole world was like a dream, an illusion, in which

---

8 Giacomo Casanova, *History of My Life,* Vol. 5, Chapter 5, p. 117.
9 *A Teaching Dedicated to the Feminine Gender,* Tape 374 ed. (Yelm: Ramtha Dialogues, 1998).
10 *Love Is a Many-Splendored Thing,* Tape 382.5.

everything and everyone we meet in our life is ultimately a mirror reflection of who we are? Ramtha expresses this simply when he says that "it is how we make love do we make life."[11] And love in the end begins with us.

---

11 *Miracles Exist Outside Emotional Time,* Tape 422 ed.

CHAPTER 3
Intimate Secrets of a Master

Running Back to Our Past in Circles

No one ever conquered me. What do you do when you have done what I have done?[1]

We did it; I did it; I love it. I am going to teach you how to do it, so listen. Outrageous? Please remember this, please: I am 35,000 years old. I have come back. I pick up my personality on the way down to the body. I pick up a consciousness of Ramtha because Ramtha was a tactician. Ramtha never got caught up in his people, he never got caught up in women, he never got caught up in drugs, he never — Well, violence, you know, I owned all of that. I mean, you know, after a while, when you are really good at it, there is no challenge in it. There is no challenge in it. So it was my first great lesson of realizing that I had owned my past.

Now there was another lesson that I shared with a few masters, about the first time I decided to march outside of Onai.

And, you know, while I was in camp there, my lady was brought to me and she was mad, and she created that scar on my face. I mean, we were only fourteen years old. I mean, please, how deep is this going to get? But we are talking about giants of people. I mean, you look like children to my image and the

1 You can find the details of Ramtha's lifetime in *Ramtha, The White Book,* and in *Ramtha, A Beginner's Guide to Creating Reality* by JZK Publishing, a division of JZK, Inc.

people of my image at that time. So sometimes, you know, you kind of look like that because you kind of are that.

And so I left. So we marched. She was sent to be taken care of and we marched. I am fourteen years old and I am really mad. And so we march and we keep marching and we keep marching and we come to another mountain range and we come back, and lo and behold if it doesn't start looking a little familiar. Well, I made a circle; I came right back where I started. I mean, that is embarrassing. That is embarrassing. I never confessed that before. That is embarrassing. Well, you know, the ruins of the city over the mountaintop start to look a little familiar. And we want to know who went there before us. And lo and behold, it is the same place I left from. I just made a big fat circle. You do it all of the time. Raise your hands if you do it. Hey, that is really embarrassing.

Well, you can imagine. You can imagine what I felt like. And everybody is going — And I am looking at them and going, "You are the ones that threw rocks at me, wanted me to come out. Don't blame me if we are back here where we started." You know, and like the song says, I thought I was so wise, but I am really stupid because at fourteen — well, you know, fourteen — I could say, "What do you expect?" But I was really a bold creature at fourteen years of age.

So listen to me. Listen. It was really embarrassing. And of course my first response is, "Well, nyah, nyah, nyah, nyah, nyah. You followed me. I mean, what do you expect?" That is how I know about victim/tyrant. I was an impressionable fourteen-year-old. So, hey, I will tell you what. After that experience — Now there was no psychology in my day. There was only — We create reality? Well, no one told me that.

So I am coming back to my first big conquest. I am coming back to the woman that I love — I am fourteen; I mean, how deep can that be? — and I am coming back to where I started from. It is only because I didn't have the wisdom to continue a straight line.

Well, you can keep coming back to the past, but let me tell you what I thought about that, the first time I did that — and the only time I did that — was I was embarrassed. I mean, I was embarrassed. I am leading an army. Yes, I am fourteen years of age. I needed that experience, but once is enough for me. Why isn't it enough for you? Why do you keep circling back to some poignant, emotional time? Because you don't have any emotion in your life, so you have got to create some. You have got to have redemption.

I can tell you something. I didn't have to go back a second time. I made a straight line out of there, and I never wanted to go back. And you just keep doing it. You just keep doing it. Why? Like mother, like daughter; like father, like son? It won't work. It won't work.

The Secret of Looking into Someone's Eyes

Listen. What keeps you from the miraculous that I have talked to you about since the beginning that I appeared here — it does — is you are holding on; you hold onto your past. What does that mean? Well, I used to tell my beginning audiences, "Look around you; does the past still exist?" And they would be a little embarrassed. No, but where it does exist is up here. You have a slice of your brain that is exclusively dedicated to your past. How many of you understand? You do?

You know why you have it there? You have said this many times, "I don't like to think about this," but you never said, "I don't like to feel about this."

You know, one of the reasons that I love the dance that I chose — listen to me — is that is going to put away a lot of your bravado. Now I chose William because William doesn't have rhythm like you do when you can run around here like a bunny on a hot plate. What he has is he has the ability to look you right in the eye. That to me, that to your Teacher is the most singular, important attribute of being close to someone because the eyes are the windows of the soul. When we have the ability to look them deep in the eye, here is a scary thing that happens: We are affecting these people. We are no longer interested in their body parts. We are looking them in the soul. We can at once be contaminated or we are going to look beyond their presentation.

The reason that I have made him demonstrate up here is — amongst all of these silly studly-do-rights in my audience, because this also shows you that we are millions and millions of years different in attitude — is this: that the dance should be a moment to where energy called music is being explored. And the partner should never be someone that can keep up rhythm with you, because that is what you do in everyday life. You want anybody in your life that can keep up with you, but do you have solitary innocence to have someone look into your soul?

How many of you watched the tapes of my teachings and when it got up close and it got to my eyes and I am suddenly looking at you, how many of you felt I was looking into your soul? Raise your hands. So be it. Why should I teach you anything other than what I am? I can only teach you what I am. I cannot teach you on objection or subjection. I can only teach you to what I know. And anyone that has ever sat across from me will know how powerful I am when I look you in the eye, because it is an uncomfortable feeling. How many of you have experienced that? So be it.

So why shouldn't I want a teacher that can teach you to do that? His greatest attribute is he can do that. What, are you ashamed? Are you afraid? Are you afraid to have someone gaze beyond who you are that is not interested in your butt, your legs, your vagina, your penis? I mean, what is it to have someone look in your eyes? It doesn't matter what color your eyes are. Mine are really black. Don't ever believe that garbage that blue eyes are prettier than black eyes, because I can outshine blue eyes any day of the week. I don't have those color eyes and I never wished that I had. I loved who I was.

Can we look in another's eye and look deep in their soul? Now that is a gift, because how do we move people? If we are not looking at their body parts but we are looking into their soul — are you listening to me? — it doesn't mean that you create a sexual tête-à-tête. It means that you are watching them. Do you know how long it has been since they have ever watched that they have been watched? That is the reason I have that dance going on. And why do I say it is beautiful? It is not the dips and all of that. What is beautiful is to have another being look at another being in the eye. And no matter who I have put with him, he has done that.

So I want you to understand something. I am Ramtha the Enlightened One. I am a 35,000-year-old being. I am heavily cloaked. I am here to embrace and then to polish your rough edges so that you shine brightly and beautifully and that your whole focus is about the teaching. It is the message, masters.

So am I doing this because I get an entertainment off of doing that? Please. Do you know how much I have seen in 35,000 years? I have seen a lot, much more — I mean, if you could dream as grand as I have seen, well, we wouldn't have any problem with you. You would be ready to go on and you would disappear out there. You just would. And your past would roll up behind you. It would just roll up; it would be gone.

But you are too involved with keeping that going. I have sent runners; I have talked; I have embarrassed you; I have said the truth to you. Most of you hide from me because you don't want me to look in your eyes, but don't you think I know who you are? You don't think that I know what you go back to or what is ahead of you? You are desperately mistaken.

I have him teach you this. Yes, I have had him dance with men. I have had him dance with old and young. I have had him show them something. No, they are not to fall in love with him, because he is not intimating any sexuality to them. He is looking into your soul. And yet the greatest love, it never had to do with body parts; it had to do with somebody who could understand us, who could see so clearly all of our illusions: our body's illusions, our face illusions, our bravado, our studly-do-right or I-am-too-good-for-you attitude, "I have too much money to dance with you because I am special," and all of that oxen dung.

No, the most memorable people that we will ever meet in our life are those that held us close and didn't look at our bodies and look how tall we are, how old we are, who we were. They looked into our soul. Now there is the fourth seal. That is the home of love; I mean real love, unconditional love, magical love. And it forced — it forced — our sexuality to be compelled there or else made us turn around and walk away. And what it shows us — I know this; I experienced this — what it shows us: It shows us not who they are but who we are not.

So when we get emotional reactions off such a dancer, such a master — We get emotional reactions off of that. I mean, we know what the swing is. It can be, "Oh, you are the greatest man or greatest woman I have ever danced with;

I am madly in love with you because no one ever looked in my soul," and all that garbage, or we have the antithesis of it. "You are not going to teach me anything, bud." I mean, can you have someone look into your eyes and after a while, in a moment, it will be romantic and hypnotic. But do you know what hypnotism is? Hypnotism is laying down the image. And that is so easy to understand, and it is an actual science because we look into the eyes of a person; we are not looking down here to you-know-what. Well, suddenly we are at once flattered and then we are disgusted. And if it keeps on, we start to go downhill. Why? Why? Because everything we think is reflected in those eyes. And an entity who doesn't care about your body, your body parts, your gender — your gender, how old you are, how young you are, how rich you are, how poor you are, you see, because those are all of your issues — can hold you till the last dance. If you can stay there and keep giving it up and giving it up and giving it up and staring back into those eyes, you have found the Holy Spirit of a person. And that is what everyone longs to have — I know I wanted it, and I know you do too — the Holy Spirit.

It is fun to play in this body, but if we play with other people who are playing in their body, we know we can never take it serious. Then they are never going to be that enlightened creature we hope that — We think we can mold them; it never works. You know why? Because we can never look in their eyes and honestly know that the knowingness gets through to them, because if anyone falls in love with our knowingness, it might mean that all the work we have put in our body may be to no avail.

Emotional versus Analytical People

Now if this is the seat, the kingdom of heaven, right here, the frontal lobe,[2] the golden seat of God, then behind it — and though this is just an analogy — it actually represents slices or compartments of thinking. And as we start here, we see that this is the bravado thinking that doesn't have a lot of emotion with it. It is more the analytical thinking. It sits right behind the frontal lobe. But as we take each slice and we go down, we begin to see something important happening.

So right behind the frontal lobe is the most analytical people in the world. And those are intellects; those are highly educated people, or they are religious people. They are politics; they are government officials; they are kings and queens. In other words — in other words — they lead the world. These are money managers. These are people that think in terms of analytical equations.

You may not think that you belong in this group, but maybe you do because not simply the people that control the world, people that are in control, period, are third-seal people. We are talking about people, mothers who are analytical who follow the mother code; fathers who are analytical that follow the banker code, the job code, the military service code, the old-fashioned code, servitude. Suppress your emotions and rule; I mean, powerful people know how to do that.

Now these people are institutionally trained. They go to school; they have learned. And who writes the history book? Who writes the psychology? Who writes the information? School is not about — There is no educational system that deals with a

2 See Fig. C: The Brain, p. 249.

person's emotions. There isn't. There is only educational systems that deal with teaching people to be robots to a manifesto of a certain criteria of how to live and how to be. How many of you understand?

So then we have a real problem because teenagers, young people, older people, I mean, they get really suppressed in their emotions, so no wonder the school system falls apart for them because they have no way to handle this growing rage, this growing feeling, this growing emotion. So they start marching, and they march for the things that are righteous and the things that they feel right about. Well, feeling right is not intellectually right. How many of you understand?

So if we go down the scale then from the slices of the brain we go down to this point, that right before the subconscious we have human beings that only can live in emotion. They only think by feelings because feelings — feelings — their evolution has been from the intellect down to "I feel it is right." Well, you know, somebody that tells you, "I feel it is right," you should say, "Baby, you feel that is right for you? Well, I would never want to be wrapped up in your emotional body because you never wake up when you are that deep in your emotions. And you don't love me. You don't care about me. You just want to have a redemption-emotional hit, whether it is feeling good, feeling bad, feeling sexual. Let's relive the moment, honey. Come on, let's do it. It was our moment. Well, what in the hell are you talking about? I have left you behind. I don't even have any footprints with you. Come knocking on my door, honey, you are a stranger."

So this is what we have. You should say, well, master, then how do we reconcile — If you say that, then what is the difference between what you are saying and an intellect? Well, an intellect is supposed to be a person that sees things purely intellectual, and that should be the emotional fulfillment, that how they rule the world should be the response of that clearly and cold-hearted intellectual observation versus a person who is bouncing off the walls, who every day you have to give to them what they want in order for them to be sane because, you see, they are not addicted to the intellect; they are addicted to chemistry. How many of you understand? Chemistry, chemicals — chemicals.

You know how I know that? Because at first you will agree with me or disagree with me, and if I keep pushing you, you will get emotional. And if I keep going any further, you get mad. And if I get any further, you will get deeper and deeper and deeper until you blow up. And then you will realize I was right. It is called levels of emotion in the brain.

Now I could call that consciousness and energy, but we really just took one — I mean, our consciousness is one line. I mean, this is what is illuminating. We are only breaking down a line of consciousness and energy into its components. We are still talking about your life, and that life is your consciousness and your energy, the consciousness which has got a name and a social security number; it has got a face and it has got a body. So the whole work we have done so far has just been about this consciousness, which is you.

And we are going to explore this consciousness to its completion. And if we can do that, then we will understand how to do this. Unfortunately what we see here, going up against the subconscious,[3] is that we see that pretty soon people don't think; they react. You don't really think. You know how I know you don't really think? Because you can't conjugate what I am saying without feeling emotionally upset about it.

---

3 The lower cerebellum. See Fig. C: The Brain, p. 249.

You know what that means? That means there is no neuronet of logical thinking at this level. There are only neurons there to turn on the water faucet of emotions. And that is where most of you have lived. You have lived by feelings, getting your feelings hurt, not being recognized for what you think you should do. So you run back to the past and you drag out all of that garbage and you start living it, because you are addicted. You are addicted to your emotional body. And you — you, you — I want you to understand that the reason we have a collapse in consciousness is because you just think with your body. Oh, and we don't need to educate you. You are just going to be a reactive creature. Anything other than that is going to be pure philosophical speculation because, you see — You know how I know that? You will say, "It doesn't feel right to me," when you are not getting the reaction you want to.

Do you know what depravity is made out of? It is going to the most depraved links and aspects and depths to get a reaction. That is why there are mass murderers. That is why there are rapists. That is why there are serial killers. That is why there are graymen. That is why there are politicians. That is why there are leads, heads of church and state. They are depraved people that go to the ends of power to secrete out of that control the emotions they need to survive on.

So you don't think this pertains to you? I will tell you how much it pertains to you: Because you are so consciously your linear life, you are Flatlanders.[4] And what is the Teacher doing? The Teacher is coming from not two dimensions but millions of dimensions and endeavoring to dimensionalize you right at the prime of your emotional, intellectual maturity.

---

4 Edwin A. Abbott, *The Annotated Flatland, A Romance of Many Dimensions* (Cambridge: Perseus Publishing, 2001).

So what does this mean? Well, this means: Do you know who you are? I will tell you who you are. You are the consciousness and energy of your name, your body, its chemical makeup, its genetics, and who you are known by. I laugh at the folly of people who think they are more beautiful than other people because it just means they are desperate old bags because old — they will never get off that line and they will never get fermented and they just have to die. That is all there is to it. You are leaves on the tree of life instead of being the tree of life itself.

The miracle exists outside of emotional time. And so obviously then the whole school, RSE,[5] has been about learning about ourselves, learning about our individual selves from our genetics to our upbringing, to our choices, and who we have finally arrived ourselves to be, and how we argue for our differences, and how we argue for that which is termed our separateness. And in fact we are arguing for our emotions; we are arguing for our limitations.

The Strange Paradox of an Amnesiac And Split Personality

What do you call amnesia? I mean, how do you define amnesia? Hey, not only are you amnesiacs, but an amnesiac within the human principle will be one who has a head injury — a head injury; this is important — that the injury actually obliterates the neuronet that was the connection to their past. What about these amnesiacs? Well, let me tell you a little bit about something about them.

If a person who is very virile, very caught up in social consciousness, very mindful of themselves, very ownful of other

---

5 Ramtha's School of Enlightenment.

persons — people, places, things, times, and events — suddenly they go out and get on their cycle and a car hits them and they have this concussion, and they wake up. And they ask them, "Well, who are you?"

They say, "I don't know." They have the motor, they have the subconscious, to answer the question, but they don't know who they are. Now don't you find that curious that they could say — Literally, the doctor says, "Who are you?" and they say, "I don't know." Well, obviously one part of the brain didn't get dented because they can answer cognitive exchanges in communication; right? They can say that, but then the doctor says, "Well, who are you?" and they say, "Well, I don't know."

That is sort of a baffling thing. I mean, they are cognizant, they heard me, they exchanged with me, but they don't know.

"Well, what is your social security number?"

They know about social security numbers, but they don't have one.

"Well, who is your family?"

"I don't know."

"Do you have a husband? Do you have a wife?"

"I don't know."

"Do you have children? Do you have next of kin? Who is your mother?"

"I don't know."

"Where did you come from?"

"I don't know."

Well, what an interesting concept medically. Now isn't that a paradox? They can answer the question but they answer it with "I don't know."

So what happens to an amnesiac? An amnesiac has an injury to their image, the brain that governs their image. So, you know, you can have a partner who is madly and passionately in love with you, and they can get hit by a big Mack truck, and did you know — the next day or ten days when they come out of their coma — did you know they won't have any feeling for you at all, baby? I mean, that is just a little disconcerting. You walk in the room, no radar love there.

So now I have to stoop to amnesia to talk to you about this. There are medical histories of people all of the time who have accidents — Accidents: They weren't castrated and go, "I don't know." I mean, they don't say that. They could have an injury to the breast. "I don't know." No, they would never say that. They would say, "This terrible thing happened to me." No, no, no, no, no. So that is body parts. The brain is still aware. But when it happens to the brain, we have got a problem because the brain can forget you overnight. The most intense, passionate lover in this audience will be an alien after the accident.

So of course the medical association wants to quickly find these people's relatives and — people, places, things, times, and events — drag them into the room. And a son can look at his mother and never recognize her. A wife can look at her husband and never know him. He will be a stranger to her.

And so what does medical science endeavor to do? Get them reacquainted with their family. But are they ever the same person? They never are, because they don't have any guilt that they don't recognize their mother. But the mother does. There are some clues going on here. They don't have any guilt that their lover recognizes them but they don't recognize their lover. And their lover tries to love them; they don't feel anything for them. Do you know why? They have no past with this person — no past.

So the miracle exists outside of emotional time. So maybe

these people were in search of a miracle. Maybe they wanted to be reincarnated but never die and never have any affliction with the association. And all we have to do is we just have to damage part of the brain. And then that is all we have to do, you know, get run over by a mail truck or dairy truck or a burger truck, whatever. That is all you have to do. It is all over with.

But what this tells us is something really marvelous and really interesting because then my teaching to you is not fantasy; it is an actuality. That means then that the most surface, tenuous parts of our being are about our past. In other words, then if a very small part of our brain was to get injured, this is the brain that keys in as a computer, that every person — every person, place, thing, time, and event — in our past and in our present is only recognized by emotion.

You know what you call people that you don't have an emotional contact with? Strangers. Well, an amnesiac recognizes its mother as a stranger. Turn to your neighbor and tell them that little paradox, please.

Now therapy has shown that the reintroduction to their family, that even when they are reintroduced to the family, here is how the family starts out. The family starts out with sympathy. So the individual endeavoring to be reinvented is reinvented on sympathy. And then everyone loves him or her and they are there, and then slowly they start to grind out their bitches. "I am so happy you are home. You know, I was so worried sick about you. I was so worried, and I went over in my mind, you know, all the things that we went through," and then they get carried off on their own carousel. I mean, this poor creature doesn't even know who they are, and suddenly they are carried off at their own memories. And then they turn around and look at them and say, "Do you understand what I am saying?"

And they look at you and go, "No."

So reintroduction to the family is a difficult thing for amnesiacs because the amnesiac has no bonding with these people. They really don't. It is sort of like taking you out of your family situation and introducing you to a bunch of aliens and saying, "You know, you had an accident, but this is who you really are."[6] How many of you understand? You do?

So what do amnesiacs and the miracle have in common? Well, if we leave an amnesiac alone, the amnesiac can manifest anything because they are so clean. I mean, they are clean.

And if you try to remake that person in the same body, you are never going to remake them. You never will. They are lost to you forever. Why? Because the past is destroyed by a neuronet that controlled the emotions in the body. And the only way we could ever re-create that neuronet is to go step by step to a person's past. And every people, place, thing, time, and event — every little event — made them who they were in your life.

How many of you understood that teaching? Hey, you listen to me. You change your attitude. There is no reason to feel sorry for yourself. You have many slices of the brain to move to. And you know how you move to them? With will. Will.

If an amnesiac can answer the doctor's questions and yet not know his roots, then we are talking clearly about an example of stages in the brain's neuronet. In order to accomplish the work, which is no-time, you have to be able to do the same thing.

What is your greatest stumbling stone? Your emotional body. Oh, you think — you think — that I am talking about guilt and unworthiness and lack and shame and all of that. No, I will

---

6 This scenario is brilliantly illustrated in the science fiction movie, *Total Recall* (Artisan Entertainment: Arnold Schwarzenegger, Sharon Stone, 1990).

tell you what I am talking about: apathy and lethargy. Apathy and lethargy, now where do those belong in the first three seals? I mean, that is a giving-up. That is indifference. We must be a complete amnesiac when it comes to focus.[7] We cannot belong to anyone. We cannot know anyone. We cannot be associated with anyone. We cannot have any emotional attachment.

Yeshua ben Joseph was a beautiful man. I mean, this was a six-foot-three, red-headed, bronzed man with blue eyes, and he had a beautiful wife, and he was willing to be fermented at thirty-three. Now fermentation: He must forget it all, so he traded that in for his Father's kingdom of heaven, because he was willing. He could already predict every emotion.

Listen to me. Your whole life is about emotion. It is about feeling good. It is about feeling bad. Imagine a life where those are not comparable to one's justification of self. Can you do that? Oh, you say you can, but I have people up here that couldn't even stand to live without each other. Can you do that, I mean, even for the kingdom of heaven? Well, no, if you tried anything, you have betrayed somebody. Well, what a frigging loss. I mean, really.

Emotions are what the amnesiac loses. That doesn't mean they won't have any in their new life. They will build them, but they will never build them on the building blocks of the past. That is the reason why wives and husbandmen go, because they don't have any past with them. Now do you have a past with the person you are with? I mean, are you having them toe the line for your own indiscretions? Are you having them toe the line for your own insecurities and your own unworthiness? Moreover — moreover — are you making them suffer because they aren't as sexual with you? Well, understanding your mind, well, you know, your mind is between your legs. Let's get real

---

7 When it comes to the practical application of the Great Work.

here. Maybe it is because they don't know how to make love to you because they in themselves don't see you that way.

We are talking about a real go-to-the-cliff-and-let's-fall-off. You are afraid of that. You are afraid of that. I mean, you worked too hard to have this image. That means — that means — that emotion is moving. It is the pendulum; it is moving, ticktock. A grandfather clock that has that pendulum is counting the hours away. And one day you will just be too old and you can't get it up and, God, who is going to take care of you then? The government. Maybe that is what it is going to be.

Hey, you don't like what I am telling you? Well, if we are here — I love God, so I am going to defend God to you, and you I know how to take care of. And I am going to tell you this: You will never be that divine moment if you live in your emotional body because your emotional body has really determined your thinking. You can't even say a statement without it inferring to some feeling.

The best conversation you could come up with is one that ends you back in bed with the person. I mean, that is the best you could do. I mean, that is a crying shame, especially if we know we are going to die because of it and not live forever. When we live by our emotions — And here is the other thing that amnesiacs have that is strange. You do the research; you will find out that they get younger and they don't understand why they do. I will tell you why they do. They don't have any emotions going. They get younger. Twenty-year-old bones turn into twenty-year-old bones.

Here is another example: a person with split personality. One personality operates on one part of the brain while the other is an amnesiac. This one personality is the outcropping of a lot of pain and suffering from the other person, or weakness, whatever you want to call it. So one personality, a split personality, is a person who feels sorry and bad and created this image, this superimage, from the image that they are living: put upon, taken advantage of, you know, "Here I am and I am going to die just to teach you a lesson."

So what happens, these kinds of people develop this other personality. Well, when the other personality goes into effect, the immune system is strengthened, and suddenly this person doesn't have sugar diabetes, they don't have sclerosis of the liver, they don't have gastrointestinal diseases, and they don't have cancer; they don't have Parkinson's disease. There is a little, tiny part of the brain that is the antithesis of the victim. That is a proven fact.

A split personality is a personality that will be its own strength and its own character and its own will. But in doing that, it nearly abolishes everyone in their life, including itself. And it doesn't have diseases. And the moment it goes back to being the normal person, then it succumbs.

Hey, you don't believe me? I am a wonderful example. The whole biorhythms of this body change in the twinkling of an eye that I take it over.[8] That is right; they do. I am a whole different cat. Now that doesn't mean I have got a split personality. But it means that, I used to say to my Dialogue crew in the old days, and some of you may remember this — but I used to say to them, and this is the most severe I used to get — "Did you know that any of you sitting in this audience, we could yank you out of that body and put a master in your body, and did you know your body will walk as God?" That was as bad as I used to get.

---

8 Stanley Krippner, Ian Wickramasekera, et al., *The Ramtha Phenomenon: Psychological, Phenomenological, and Geomagnetic Data,* in *The Journal of the American Society for Psychical Research,* Vol. 92, No. 1, January 1998.

That was pretty bad. So I am telling you again today, and we have gotten really bad.

So what does it mean then? An amnesiac that destroys a center of the brain through injury, a split personality that doesn't use that center of the brain and uses a different center of the brain to create a whole different entity, they are never subject to the rules biologically that the entity that they used to be are subject to. How many of you understand? You don't believe me? Go do the medical research yourself, please. There are halls of books for you to read.[9]

So what does this say then? A miracle exists outside — (Audience: Of the emotional body.) You got it. So if we had an amnesiac come to this audience, I don't care how awful — They could be Hitler; I don't care. If he is an amnesiac, he will never know he was ever Hitler. It will take the trials, and then again he will feel victimized because he cannot remember ever doing it. How many of you understand? He could learn to come and be a master.

Totally Present in the Moment of Making Love

This is what you do. You have a thought — your educational system, your parents, your DNA — but you have only been educated so far. I mean, you have been educated, well, half the size of this little fingernail, and look how many more we have got left. But from that — from that — then the experience, hot and cold and good and bad, emerged. Then by the time that you are sexual creatures, sexual maturity, good and bad really starts to take over and be confusing.

---

9 For further research in this field, see the authoritative work by Colin A. Ross, *Dissociative Identity Disorder: Diagnosis, Clinical Features, and Treatment of Multiple Personality,* 2nd. Edition (New York: John Wiley & Sons, 1996).

So what did you do? You are in a body. You are in a body, a chemical body. Forget the brain. You are in a chemical body that is responding to decisions. And it is not just the megadecisions; it is the little decision to sit here and be stupid. That is a decision too. You decided to live, to swing from tree to tree off of your emotional body. You are just swinging.

So how could we explain better time than if we explain it according to our expectation of feeling? We wake up in the morning, we are totally innocent, and then we go about being in time. We go about feeling. We go about feeling. Get up out of that warm bed. First, now we know it is warm; now we know the temperature is cold. It is warm; that is our first emotional feeling. Then our bladder is full and we have got to get up and race over there to the latrine. And we race to the latrine and we urinate. We are urinating into water, and we are sitting there and we are urinating, and the next thing we do is we go look in the mirror to see who it is that was urinating. It is true.

Our lives — your life, and my life in the beginning — were based upon feeling. Mine was based upon anger. Yours is based upon feeling and redemption. And you have got this all confused with love. You think that being true to those emotions is love. But you are so wrongo in the Congo.

So, hey, is it any wonder I say consciousness and energy creates reality? Here we have alpha and we have omega, and in between we have time. Time can only happen if in our mind — if in our mind — We never accept what is in our mind until we have felt it. If we have to feel it, then it is thrown into time and then we go through the whole biological system of feeling it. We were originally created to have the consciousness — and, remember, we have got to make known the unknown — to have the thought, and then to feel not only as the Observer who creates energy and creates this drama, these props, these people, places, things, times, and events but then we must have the body ready to experience people, places, things, times, and events. Every one of those criteria we have an emotional hitch to.

And how — how — do we determine the deepest emotional hitch? How do we know we are operating from the first three seals? Because the people, places, things, times, and events in our life will be geared predominantly to one of those three.

An amnesiac then would be like a virgin. It really would be. The first time they ever made love, the instincts of making love would come over but they would have no fantasy, so it would be a pure moment. Pure moment, that is the virgin — the pure moment.

You aren't going to like the following teaching, but so what? We want to become an amnesiac so that we can be reborn and our body can be transcended.

So Yeshua ben Joseph's mother was a virgin, but not a virgin in the context we are talking about, a virgin in the pure moment of experience.

So Mary then was really a virgin in mind. She had no past in making love, no experience in making love. So her child was conceived through the purity of the Now. Remember, the miracle exists outside of emotional time. So if she has no affiliation to the moment, she is like an amnesiac. And it is going to come. That moment is going to come and it is going to be powerful and wonderful, and you will — I don't have to tell you. You know the musk and the odor and the love and the passion that comes when you are in the moment. Well, that is called the virgin moment, and we could only conceive brilliance in such a moment.

Now the reason that men — and I am going to call you on this in a moment, but bear with me — the reason why men never married harlots is because harlots could always take their seed from them but without responsibility. They never wanted a harlot to bear a child because instinctively they were never virgin in their mind.

Now this is the matriarchal — or is it matriarchal or patriarchal? This is the male-dominated world of religion. Those terms happened long after me. But this was the world of religion and politics and government where women were cattle so — I mean, really cattle. And I have a lot of women in this audience that need to hear this teaching about the miraculous, that men do have, and women too, a really deep knowingness that goes back to their Holy Spirit; that when we are there and set to bear a child, we do not want to bear the child in decadence because if consciousness and energy is across the board, and it is, then even ovulation, the eggs that are going to come down are going to be equal to our fantasy, our mind; the sperm that comes out of us is going to be equal to our mind. So what do we end up, in the fruit of the womb? We end up to a really decadent human that is coming here and they are going to be rotten, and they are going to be just like you, except they are going to live it openly while you live it secretly.

Then we have the opposite problem. We have the opposite problem of an ovulating partner who fantasizes not to the decadence but to the extreme of enlightenment. They are making love in God. They are making love to a saint. They are making love to something, and that calls out within them the highest order of their seed, because don't ever tell me and don't ever show your ignorance to say that a man's semen, his spermatozoa — are you listening to me? — that it is a random shot, because what causes the strongest to penetrate that egg is going to be the strongest that is supported by the mind of its creator.

So what a man thinks, how he reacts with his woman, that whole dynamic, if it is done just wham-bam-thank-you-ma'am — You know, most of the women in this audience find really their husbands disgusting because they are not romantics; they are not intimate. They don't even know the first clue about the sacred. What is the sacred? All a sacred rite is, is to diffuse and turn into magic the emotions into a moment. There is nothing more important and more powerful than the moment. When we have slam-bam-thank-you-ma'am, clearly — listen, ladies, and listen, men — clearly, you have a lot of lackluster to your spiritual self. You don't want a man like that and, moreover, you don't want a woman like that, you don't, because what makes love magical is not the act but the sacred that leads to the act, because it is all mind.

CHAPTER 4
Don Juan and Saint-Germain
at the Countess' House

Two Unusual Guests

There is a really, really famous story, a very famous story that happened in France, in the countess' house where there were a bunch of illustrious guests invited, and one of those guests was Saint-Germain, the ultimate alchemist. Well, he drove up in a carriage that was very plain, a brougham carriage, but his carriage had a lot of modern conveniences to it: a flop-down table in the back, a heating element, a driver that had been with him for two hundred years. I mean, it was, you know, this was a top-of-the-line model.

And he walks in. He is a little man, and he isn't really a very handsome man, and he wears all black, black velvet. But he has buttons that instead of making them out of humble seashells, they are made out of diamonds, and the suckers are that big — buttons. Basic black and diamonds go a long way, the garment of the master. He has black silk stockings on. He has black velvet shoes and he has diamond buckles on them. He has lace at the end of his sleeves, the rarest, most beautiful Spanish lace that had ever been made, and he has a hanky tucked right there. You know, we only wore hankies because things smelled bad in those days and/or we sniffed snuff and we didn't want it running down into our beautiful maroon lips. I mean, brown running into maroon is not a pretty color. So that is why we had a hanky right there.

So he gets out and he comes to dinner. And he really isn't interested in any of the food they have because he is such an enlightened, up-on-it, riding-with-mind being. I mean, all of that wealth that he has, he made that wealth. He didn't work for it; he made it. So it doesn't matter.

He was a little man. He had a wonderful hairdo, coiffure. And here are all these beautiful women — beautiful women — in their bustles and their gowns and pearls all around and powdered things on top of their head; I mean, really it was a sight to behold. And all we have to do is add candlelight and then we really get the flashing of those stones.

The other favored guest there was Don Juan. Well, Don Juan ends up coming there, and he is all atmosphere with wintergreen velvet brocade and gold. We have some problems. He is all, you know, deep green with gold brocade and lace at his neck and, of course, the cuffs and, of course, his hanky. And let me see if I can recall his buttons. Well, they weren't diamonds. Well, it will come to me later. And he has bloomers on and then he has stockings and he has green velvet brocade heels on. And he has black oiled hair and it is tied with a pink satin bow. Oh, lordy. And the atmosphere he brought in, we thought we were experiencing a thousand nights of jasmine.

So here we have two real masters sitting at the table: Saint-Germain, beautiful, austere, simple black velvet and diamonds accented with white lace, and then we have the gaudy Don Juan sitting down the table. And he is a little unhappy because Saint-Germain is raining on his parade. Not only does Saint-Germain not eat the seventeen-course meal as Don Juan did, he doesn't even drink the sherry that is offered. He is asking for the deepest burgundy they have got. What does he eat? He eats simple oats in hot water and drinks wine.

So now this is a very classical and recorded — recorded — incident in history.[1] So here we have the most illustrious guests of the time. So who is it going to be? Are the ladies of the table going to be involved with Don Juan? And here was Don Juan's greatest attribute. He couldn't help himself. What made him such a fantastic lover is because it wasn't that he was so good in bed, wham-bam-thank-you-ma'am; it was that he could look into a woman's eyes and converse with them and never look away, and never be impatient, and hold the moment. And every woman — every woman — he ever looked, he seduced, and not that he wanted to. It is just that that part here was a cascade to you-know-where. That is what made him famous. And men hated him. They despised him. They talked about him behind his back. He still showed up at dinner in wintergreen velvet and gold brocade. He had an ability. He had an ability. He knew how to make every person in his sight the only person in the world.

When men make love to women, it is almost as if they — Sometimes the women think that they might as well just have a hole in the wall and go for it. And then they get the awful feeling that comes to them in that most susceptible state that their husbandmen or their lovers are not really making love to them. That is true. But he didn't have that problem. He knew

---

1 Giacomo Casanova, *History of My Life*, Vol. 5, Chapter 5, p. 116: "The dinner which I found most entertaining was the one to which she [Madame d'Urfé] invited Madame de Gergy, who came with the famous adventurer, the Count of Saint-Germain. Instead of eating he talked from the beginning to the end of dinner; and I listened with the greatest attention, for no one was a better talker. He made himself out to be a prodigy in everything, he aimed to amaze, and he really amazed. His tone was peremptory, but no one took it amiss, for he was learned, speaking all languages well, a great musician, a great chemist, with an attractive face and the ability to win the friendship of all women. . . ."

exactly how to do it, and it was his gift. And he made love to the most beautiful women in Europe and the ugliest women in Europe. But if you asked him, he doesn't even remember what they looked like. He doesn't. That is his claim to fame. That is why he was Don Juan, because all he had to do was look into those eyes and hold that gaze and he knew the soul of the person, and from that, intimacy flowered. It was beautiful.

So here we have a God with a reputation of being a seducer, but a seducer that is much more than just "give me a hole in the wall and I will masturbate off of it." I mean, this man understood something. He was not a sexual man. He was a mental man that went sexual.

Now ninety-nine percent of the men in this audience don't know how to make love. And this is talking to one that never did do that, but I know what Don Juan's great gift was. It is because the way you make love is that you start with love, and if you focus on a person, you will find everything beautiful about them. But if you don't focus on them, you will only find flashes of images, and those images are the image of seduction. He seduced the intimacy of a person, not their body, and that, my friends, is what made him a master. Was he married? Yes, he was married. Did he continue along his ways? Yes, he did. His son and daughter, how beautiful were they? Exquisitely, because in the moment he made love to their mother, he was all-present and this mother was all-beautiful.

What Women Want

If you were all dressed up in your finest silks and pearls, your finest, finest lace, your finest heels, your finest buckles, and your oriental fans, and you were at a dinner, which of those illustrious guests would you be listening to: the man in black velvet with diamonds or the renowned lover? Now it becomes really obvious the division at the table, because Saint-Germain — and I mean this is an ancient master, and he is beautiful; I mean, he is beautiful — his aura, his atmosphere is powerful, and then we have a man that just knows how to seduce. So who does, at this dinner party — the only one they ever had where they were both guests — who does not only the royalty at the table but the ladies at the table listen to? Saint-Germain.

So angry was Don Juan after that that he called Saint-Germain a charlatan. Well, you know. You know what it is like. If you are rebuffed, then that person has got to be much lower than you. They could never be as glorious as you, because if you face the truth, the fact is they were greater than you, and he would never, ever accept that reality. So he wrote very horrible things about Saint-Germain, and that is how we know Saint-Germain was an actual being, because of the jealousy of Don Juan. That is how we know. We know it by emotions. How many of you understand?

Now if you can find the memoirs of Don Juan, and it is all of the volumes that he wrote in his later life, there it will be.[2] That is how you will know there was once a living master that transcended the Middle Ages into the ages of enlightenment. And that was Saint-Germain, a master — a master. You can intrigue women and men with your prowess of focus, but you could take that focus two ways, and there are two paths on this board: You could take them to your own facilitation, you can take them to your own use, you can take them to your own emotion, or you can do the opposite. You can take them to the

---

2 See Giacomo Casanova, Chevalier de Seingalt, *History of My Life*, *translated by Willard R. Trask, 12 Vols. (New York: Harcourt, Brace & World, Inc., 1966)*.

land of the mystical, the land of magic, the land of eternal life, the land of Merlin.

And every woman at that table was fascinated with the little man in the black velvet, the diamond buttons, the diamond buckles, and his stories. And every one of those women wanted a vial of eternal youth. And if they had the vial of eternal youth versus a night spent with — what is his name? — Don Juan, which one do you think they took? Turn to your neighbor and explain. I am making my point very well here.

Thank you very much, Don Juan, for writing about your jealousy, your envy, and calling Saint-Germain salacious, because without your very basic human emotion, we would have disregarded your biography, or autobiography, as fantasy. But because you were so emotional and so hostile to him, he must exist.

Oh, there are so many points being made here, my beauties. So what do women want? You think they want a vial?

So here is my point, and I have a lot of them to make here. But my point is — my points, plural, are this — that when it comes down to it, that what no man can give any woman is immortal life. And it is the fascination of women, who are already ahead of basic men, to want and desire that. And so who are they going to listen to, the greatest lover of their age or immortality? And they listened to him. And he was gracious enough to give the hostess of that dinner a vial. But unfortunately she had an engagement that day, and her maid, who had a headache, took the vial and within three hours became thirty years younger. It is magic.

This is all a true story. The countess came back, wanted to boot out the intruder — the intruder happened to have been her maid; she booted her out anyway — because she took her vial.

She sent extensive, extensive opportunities for Saint-Germain to come back. He came back once before, never gave her a vial. And of course his antithesis and antagonist, Don Juan, didn't show up because if Saint-Germain was invited, he wasn't going to come. Well, Saint-Germain, baby, this is for you.

Sexual Fantasies, Secrets Out in the Open

If men have a plethora of all humanity in their semen and they are just so stupid and they just disregard it — I mean, they are kind of like a God who really has, within the seed of their soul, every human personality available. And now we begin to see why it is unwise to just keep disregarding that so you can get a little orgasm. Well, you need it, you need it, you need it. Oh, poor thing. I mean, have you ever thought about raising your energy? Well, no. That is a different teaching, now isn't it? So what happens — and here is something interesting; you listen to this — and that is the reason why some of you are in this audience, others of you totally different: Only a very handful of you are here because your father made love to your mother in a really sacred ceremony of romance that led up — because, you see, the ceremony is to address the emotions, the antagonist.

Now where was I? Oh, yes, this, that the ceremony — Making love isn't about, well, we finished dinner, let's brush our teeth, take a shower, and hop in bed naked and get out the hairdryer and the vibrator and anything else that is going to make us feel really good. I mean, that is bad. I want to tell you something: That is bad. That isn't sacred. That isn't sacred. That is technology.

Listen, a Don Juan will know how to start getting the moment going. And it will start at about noon, bringing flowers and sharing the moment and eating together without any distraction, and looking into those eyes. This is the one thing he knows how to do really beautifully. You look in their eyes and, you know, if you do that, a metamorphosis happens. It is not only that I am working up to a night at the races but at the moment I am looking into this person's eyes, I suddenly am caught in an unemotional state of knowingness.

And then the rest of the afternoon goes on. Well, you can imagine the activity in the household. I mean, everyone is fanning themselves because it is hot in that place and, I mean, the whole afternoon is set, that the afternoon is starting to collapse to the moment. So a whole lifetime is spent to the moment, in preparation. When the moment comes, it should be slow and easy and beautiful. And we should start always from the face downward, never downward to the face, because no one ever looks at their lover after that. I know; I have watched centuries of this copulation experience.

What kind of children come through? Well, when you don't do it right, then you have — Men: Men are really decadent creatures when it comes to fantasy, because they have a million souls and so they don't know who to fantasize about. So they usually end up fantasizing about the most decadent of all of them. Anytime men fantasize about homosexual experiences — they are actually making love to a woman and they think they are making love to a man — the sperm that is going to go to that egg, you tell me what happens after that.

How many of you does this make sense to? Raise your hand. So be it, because if it does, then we can move on and we can go further.

118

And, yes, this is humiliating stuff. And it also is doing some other things. It is destroying personal people's power in this audience over you. Well, I like doing that. Well, let me tell you something about my father. I never knew my father. But my father was an Atlatian, my mother a Lemurian. I got my height from my mother and I got my tremendous mind of understanding my enemy from my father. But I got courage from my mother. So that little love match — And he took my mother, my beloved mother, and he was overcoming a great woman and he loved it. He was like an animal. And I was conceived from his sperm. Well, he conceived the devil, because I am bigger and badder and I have taken both cultures and I am going to ruin you. He created, in his lust, me, my first incarnation. It is the virgin. I am innocent. I don't know. I am ready to come. Now it is my body.

Well, if my father was an Atlatian, guess who I laid siege to? Atlatia. I was their worst nightmare. When the old cities are raised, you will see the history of the Ram written and the day of terror that came down on them. And I was the son of an Atlatian. And I got my height from my mother. It was my mother who stayed with me. And it was my ferocious mind and anger that turned back on them. That is why I know what I am talking about. Well, I was — No Atlatian was ever aggressive like me. Where in the hell do you think I got it from? From a sperm. That man just made the devil.

Who are you? I will tell you. Most of you were conceived in fantasy. You were just conceived in basic sex. You were conceived not because your father was looking into your mother's eyes. And had he been doing that, and had he done it right, you wouldn't even be here today. Got the picture? Oh, I know you don't like it. I know you don't like it. But listen. We have to also take credit for something. This was the body that was made for us. I mean, of the millions of couples, millions, billions that are copulating when you are ready to come in — I mean, what is your soul's agenda? — what body are you going to go to? Are you going to go to the body that is the antithesis of the soul? If consciousness and energy creates reality, we are going directly to a body that is equal to who we are.

So you are a crossover? It is because your old man was while he was making love to your mother. Hey, you don't like that? Well, here is something worse. Your mother was making love to another woman when she conceived you, while her husband was giving her the sperm. You don't like that? You don't like that? Then you are ignorant people because you have not taken the teaching to its lowest denominator. Sperms are not random; eggs are not random. They are who we are.

Why do you think that it was very, very important that a woman be a virgin and unexperienced to a king who wanted to create a kingdom? He didn't want her interfering with what his plans were, his legacy. I mean, wake up, please. No man wants a child from a harlot because intrinsically he knows he doesn't know. He knows that she is not making love with him. He knows she is doing it for survival. So what kind of child is going to come out of that union? Somebody that is going to come back and cut his head off. That is the story of the Caesars, in case you are interested.[3]

How many of you understand so far? You do? So what is the concept of morality? Is morality simply relative to the level on which you are existing upon? Of course it is. Is there a higher morality? Always. What is morality? Morality is a word

---

3 Suetonius, *The Lives of the Caesars*, Loeb Classical Library ed., trans. by J.C. Rolfe, 2 vols. (Cambridge: Harvard University Press, 1914).

that stems from the moral of the story. It is the moral of the fantasy; this is the truth. This is who we spawn. Your children — your children — your greatest nightmares were created by one of you, either you or your husbandman. And one of you were having a fantasy at the moment of that child's conception. The only way that soul, troubled and debased, could come in is because one of you was debased and troubled. And a man — a woman has one egg — a man has millions of opportunities.

The morality then doesn't sit entirely upon the woman, but it does if she keeps choosing the wrong partner and she keeps trying to act like a fantasy of that partner. We should love what we are. We should love that we are a woman, we should love that we are a man, and that when we are a balanced system of consciousness, disease can never eat away at our bones, our heart, our liver, our body. When we are imbalanced — imbalanced — if we are negative to negative and positive to positive, or we are positive and negative swinging, it only takes a moment of imbalance for a seed — just like we bring a child in the world — for a seed of disease to also be fostered into the world.

You know, there is this wonderful mystery in science and medicine. It is a mystery. And the only reason they acknowledge that is because their hypotheses of how venereal diseases happen, that there are some people who are absolutely immune to them, and whether it is syphilis, whether it is genital warts, whether it is gonorrhea, whether it is cancer of the uterus, whether it is AIDS, that there are certain people that no matter how much you expose them, they never get it. In other words, these diseases really come from imbalanced, conscious people. That is where they come from, and they are passed on.

I mean, you can say, well, you know, I am a really balanced person. But when you put people in the sex act and you watch their fantasies, it is really bizarre what they do, what they think, how debased they will do to become. It is that imbalance that is the shorting mechanism that makes a weak first center and makes a weak first center for diseases. There are some people that no matter what you expose them to, they never get it. You know what medical science's explanation is, is that these are people that are preservable by nature. They absolutely are, because it is not their consciousness. They are not the one doing the thinking. They are not the ones doing the fantasizing. They just aren't. So if both get it, both are doing it.

That is all right. Every organism, every life organism, is sort of like we come together and we copulate and we bring a child in the world — correct? — or we copulate and we just do bonding. We do the Don-Juan-look-in-your-eye, lay-down-I-think-I-love-you, and so then we can solve all problems with that act. But in reality we should never have to solve all problems with that act, because then that becomes an overused consciousness and energy and body faculty.

I mean, can your partner love you if you were abstinent? I mean, that is a good question, isn't it? And then if they can't, then you have to look at them and understand that maybe the attraction was there for what you could continuously give. Well, that is no different than the miracle exists outside of emotional time. Well, unconditional love also exists outside of emotional time. Now how do we know if somebody really loves us? If suddenly we are castrated or we can't make love any longer, will they still love us, will they still be true to us, or will they be driven to another partner?

People who are protected by nature are really not protected by nature in the sense that they are very evolved creatures.

And they are just not subject to it and it is not where their consciousness is and they don't fantasize about such things. They live in the moment; they are sincere. They are coming from a higher authority than their first seal. In other words, the eyes make the contact. And so making love is really a surrender of trust of intimacy, of that soul contact.

Well, how do we explain someone that doesn't get these things? They are not sexual people; that is how we can explain it. And if they do get it, then I think they finally realize that they are. There is nothing wrong with that. But inasmuch as we have sexual contact to create another sentient being, if we don't copulate to create another sentient being, we will create another lifeform.

So there are a lot of you in this audience that have given birth to other organisms. They are your children. They live with you from your fantasies before. They are organisms. They are alive. They have a life span. So what do you do when you come to a person that doesn't have any of those things? First off, you have to love them. You have to love them more than the creature that you are trying to make them into in your past, because anytime they become a past creature to you, then they are subject to those diseases. I want you to never forget that. The miracle exists outside of emotional time. Love and healing exist outside of our past emotions that keep up our diseases, our venereal diseases, and their cycles.

You just try this experiment. You go back to your fantasies. Try making love one time in the fantasies that spawned these diseases, and you watch the eruption happen. They belong in consciousness. If ever there was a strict teacher, it is going to be that teacher to you, and I will just have been the wind. You try it. If you do not believe me, I want you to know what I am teaching you is the truth.

How many of you have learned? Painful, but it is the reality. It is one of the things that blocks the miracle in your life because, see, your whole identity now is Don Juan emotions. And your diseases keep being brought cyclically to your present through your fantasies. Don't ever tell me something just happens to you. I will never, ever buy that. I know that somewhere while you were quiet, I have watched you have the fantasy, and there it is. You create reality. That is why you are God, for God's sake. That is why you are God.

So emotion is: We should have had the thought, we collapsed the reality, we prepared the body chemically, and then we engaged it, and then we got a rush of information chemically and electrically back to the brain. It tasted good, so we wanted to do it again, except the next time we did it, we had to do it a little harder because, you see, no original experience will ever be the same from its origin. It will always have to evolve from it. That is why people get decadent, because they start out with the virgin concept, the sacred and the intimate and all of that. But the first time — And then the second time they have to add something to it, so they keep building this cake, all of these spices that keep going in it, and pretty soon we can't even enjoy the cake because it doesn't give us the same experience. Why doesn't it give us the same experience? Because we are evolving Gods, I mean, that the nature of our life force is to make known the unknown. We could never really ever have the same experience twice. We have got to always modify it. The truth is that you keep wearing out the experience. You wear out the experience.

A man makes love to a hetaera really gifted in the art of making love; it is fabulous. I mean, his poor wife that bore him all those children, she can't do this. But if she didn't bear him children and was a hetaera, she could do the same thing. But the second time you visit the hetaera she has changed clothes and incense and she has oiled her body differently because it is going to be a new experience. That is what hetaerae know how to do. But even hetaerae get boring because that is the best you can do, baby. And one day they are traded in for a virgin. Sometimes you want the experience that isn't so clever and so devised and so propped. How many of you understand?

An end comes to all emotions because emotions are born in time. They have a time life span, and then they wear out. Boredom is when you have experienced it. So it is a new day — right, wonderful — so then you are going to start out and you are going to be a little different today. Ah, that is a little exciting. You find your lover doesn't want to stay in bed with you all day long, because they want to get out and do things. They want to be different, so you have to get out and do them. Then when you go to bed at night, it is exciting. So every day you have to keep changing to keep up with your lover. What about you? You know, what are you in it for, for the ride, for the money, for the celebration because of your children? What a pitiful thing.

What about you? So you decide to do something else. You do it three days in a row and your lover will follow you, and they will go and do that and then they don't like it. But you found yourself liking everything they did. Now you have got a little problem going on. Now the emotions change. Now we are not so quick to give ourselves because they don't understand us, they don't love for us, and they don't care for us. They only do on their condition, but we are the one that agreed to it.

I mean, these are big hooks that are sitting in you. And why am I spending all this beautiful day talking about it?

Because the reason I cannot get you to manifest a Toyota or a bucket of gold or eternal life is because you are still using these teachings as the same way that you have used all of your emotional body, and it just doesn't work. It just doesn't work. I mean, you can't persuade God to make love to you. You can't persuade God. You can't be a hetaera to God. You can't promise. You can't think you will be good, you will be all those things that religion says you will — you can't do that —and then are going to go out there and manifest. This is a whole different cat, and this is your creator. This is not some babble. How many of you understand?

Now every emotional experience, if we become addicted to it, it is important that we alter it every single time because that is our addiction. We alter it. And that can be sex, that can be pain, and that can be power. And there are people that are addicted to all three of them. They don't even care about who they are with. They just want the addiction.

Now I can tell you, and I will tell you right now that you are addicted to your emotions. We don't have to worry about wine and smoking a pipe, baby. We have got more serious difficulties. If and only if we want to be a master and have eternal life, we have serious difficulties. If we don't want those things and we are immersed in feeling good, then we just have life — life, death, and taxes.

So the reason that Saint-Germain captured the ladies at the table and the men, because he was a master of that which both could enjoy. That was a mystery. Having sex is not a mystery. And many of you are born to where both of your parents finally become love partners and then the line of who you are becomes blurred by your fantasy. I mean, you have to ask yourself, does your husband really love you when you have agreed to become a sadist or a masochist or a man? I mean, who — who — is he in love with? And this becomes very disturbing to the female mind because, yes, the first time will be fun and exciting but after a while you begin to feel a little uneasy about this, because in reality it means that you are having to play a part that, yes, in the beginning was all right but now it is becoming addictive. How many of you ladies have experienced that? Raise your hand. Look around, men.

Do you want to know why women have insecurities in a relationship? Because you make them that way. It is not just good enough. You know why? Because you are the one that has lost the art of the sacred, and it is slam-bam-thank-you-ma'am, as if you were really a special creature. They don't even know that you are unspecial. Yes, you hold a million souls in one ejaculation, but what is that worth? No wonder they don't want to get pregnant with you, because after a while they feel insecure. You know why they feel insecure? Because the only time you look forward to really being with them is when they can transcend their female and be some monster, some man, and offer their rectum to you. It is nice then, but you are going to have problems because then this lady is going to finally realize she is not with anyone that is in love with her, and she is going to have a lot of problem with her own emotional commitment with you. But eventually she will replace you because she is going to look for somebody who can just fall in love with her and look her in those eyes and make love to her — and not a phantom, not a man, not another woman, not a beast, not a fowl — just her. And if we ever find that creature, we are going to fall madly in love with them. We don't care how young or how old they are.

So why did Saint-Germain hold the table that Don Juan was so resentful of? Because he held a promise and an adventure to every human being sitting at the table; that even that the greatest prowess of the greatest lover there, he couldn't even do that. And yet this master was a master of the mind, a master of eternal life. Everyone would trade him for a vial of eternal life. That just shows you. So who is not in your life? Who isn't in your life? Who are you not, and who are you?

Our Light Review's Shocking Revelations

What does this lead to? I mean, these are all the things you will see in the light.[4] What does this lead to? Well, I want to ask you a question: How quickly does your wife want to have a baby with you when she knows what you expect her to do to you? Now how quickly does your husbandman or your lover want to have a child with you when he knows what you do and think with him? Because you know where child abuse comes from? It comes from the fantasy creating such children. Fathers rape their daughters because that is a fantasy the husband and wife end up having. They do. You don't believe me? Die, go to the light, come back, and teach this audience. Wives are envious of their daughters because their daughters are born of their husband's fantasy. They came from his sperm. How many of you understand? Sons — sons — that are there have an unusual attachment to the mother and an unusual attachment to the father. And sometimes they are even abused sexually by the father. Where do you think — I mean, I know how many of you have had child abuse in your life, and you are asking "why me?" I will tell you why you, because you came into parents that did that, and you are the secular reason for that abuse because they conceived you in that.

---

4 In the life review after death.

I love my Physician. He is sitting over here shaking his head. He doesn't disagree with me. It is all equated and he understands it, and all he can say is that is sad. Yes, it is. We always create reality. Don't let any magazine or any television show or any human being tell you that that is just human nature. Yes, we can be irresponsible, but wisdom is for us. We don't come together with another human being unless we have the wisdom to fully engage a relationship with another human being who we expect to be equally wise, that we have already gone through those childish amours and those silly fantasies. And then we come together with another person, that the reason we do is we are not coming together with a fantasy; we don't want to bear a demon from a distortion. And we can easily do that, easily.

So what is morality? Morality is saying, "No, I am not ready for a relationship. And I am not ready to give my seed, and I am not really ready to be responsible enough to share love because the truth is when I make love to you, oftentimes if you saw what I had to make love to in my mind, you would pack your bags and you would be out of here. And equally if I saw it, I would be frightened as well. So why are we doing this? Shouldn't we be in love and shouldn't we have transcended our emotions to a point where the miracle of love can happen?"

Love can only happen if there is no past. And you know what? I just wrote the key up here with Blue Body, that the way that miracles happen is when we do not base a relationship upon how we used to have sex, how we used to make love, and how we used to fantasize and think.

You think it is horrible that a little, innocent girl is raped and abused by her father or her uncle? Well, let's talk about that. The father brought that into being because he created her from the dust of his dust. She can only be in his mind what he made her to be, and that is what we have to pay a thousand lifetimes for, that no one has ever taught us we are wrong in thinking that way, because they want to be popular and they want to be sexual and they want to be accepted, and they live hypocrisies. At one point they are seductors and then they are going like this. No, no, no, no, no. Listen to me. Well, please, what are we saying? What signals are we talking about?

We want to come together in a miracle of love. Love doesn't have a past. It has to create its own Now.

So if you are still wrestling with your sexual life and these monsters up here,[5] then you are never going to hear a word that I have to teach to you because you will think that is your prerogative. And in fact today was about reaching into your mind and into your soul and into your intent and dragging those suckers out. Well, I don't care who you are. If you don't do that, you will never know the miracle, you will never know the moment, and you will never know love.

But what do we have to be ashamed of? What we have to be ashamed of is that this is the secret part of ourself we have never mastered, because we think that sex has nothing to do with us being a good man or a good woman but in fact has everything to do with it. It is the first seal, and it is how we react there is how we are going to react everywhere else.

So we started at the first seal about the miracle, and we get to see then — we get to see — that really our children embody the fantasies that we created while we were having sex. Why should that be exempt? You got another explanation for it? Well, then if you say that is exempt, then I am going to ask you who is the God that created that exemption, and shouldn't we be talking to the God of sex?

---

5 In our head.

There are men and women in this audience that said they could never have children. The fact is they didn't want them. They didn't want the responsibility. They wanted the freedom to be whoever they wanted to be without penalty. And the truth is they would not have made good parents.

So we conceive greatness, we must be in love with greatness. We consume power, conceive power, we must conceive power. It goes all the way down the line. How many of you understand?

Now I know this is a heavy teaching, but I want to ask you something: Don't you know that is what I see when I look at you? I mean, how can I tell you? You don't want me to tell you why you can't do the wonderful?

So then we go all the way back then to that old-fogy thought: morality, clean thoughts, making love cleanly, the virgin bed, the marriage bed. But we only got married because we were madly in love with one another, madly in love with one another. In other words, that look in the eye and that reach in the soul, that embrace to the mind, that carrying away of our soul, that was energy born here that moved down instead of energy that is cropped down here that will never get up here. You know, those old-fashioned principles are alive today. They were alive in my time. I mean, they are really old-fashioned.

You want a great child? Wait and fall in love, that every time — Love needs no evolution; it is. Sex needs evolution. That is the body parts that look so good. But, you know, when you fall in love with a person, always it will never really be for what they look like. It will be for their mind. And their mind is obvious — their soul, their sweetness, their beauty — the beauty of the mind. That is who we want to have children with because that is going to create the great children, the really great children.

So, you know, you can keep playing around and keep monkeying around and keep being funky, you know, and be just an old, broken-down child, or you can be a young, forever being. Broken-down children have spilt all of their life force, millions and millions and millions and millions of souls, demons, spread out on the sheets. That is a broken-down old man; that is a broken-down old woman. Or you can have and understand that miracles happen, and miracles happen because the only way that we would get in trouble is if we were doing it because of its emotional, chemical feeling.

So now it becomes very obvious then, going back to Saint-Germain and Don Juan, is that Saint-Germain didn't make a pass at anyone at the table. In fact he didn't even eat seventeen courses. He wasn't even — He didn't have any of the food, but he drank their wine. And that was the condition. Listen. He said, "I will only come if you don't feed me that awful stuff you eat." That is what he said.

"No problem. You just come."

Well, he didn't do it. So when everyone is feeding their face and breaking out with, you know, pockmarks, he is telling stories. He is beautiful; he is wonderful. You think the host was mad because he didn't eat the food? That was the only way he would come. He was honest, a great and rare trademark. He was honest.

"No, but I will wear my best finery." Black velvet with diamond buttons, Spanish lace out of those sleeves, pretty hot-looking.

So in the end, I mean, he became the most sought-after parlor guest of anyone's parlor there was in his time, because he was magical. And all the people who were jealous called him charlatan, but he was magical. What did he do? Well, he told their fortunes. He looked at them and told their prophecy. And you know what? It was dead-on. Remember, this is the court of Marie Antoinette. Dead-on. Wear your best.

So, masters, he is an enigma even today. He is coming out of rest. He will be back, but not to tell you the time, in case anyone says they are channeling him because they never will channel him. He will be his own being.

So let me get back to this. And here is the analogy. The analogy is this, that human existence is so bored and does not have a code of morality nor even a desire to achieve it, because there is no reason to achieve it, because what is on the other end of it? What is at the end of this good life, heaven and hell, you know, weighing the heart, or as the Buddha said — as Father explained so beautifully — nothing? I mean, I want you to know something. There are kingdoms that are so massive.

I don't think you are bad. I mean, you create children that are your nemesis. I mean, I don't have to tell you. I mean, you are already in it. You don't create children, you haven't made it, because you don't want to make your body big? Don't you ever, ever listen to anybody who says that they couldn't have it. No, they could. They just wanted to play — are you with me? — because I listen to their excuses and I just look at them and smile. Because in one sense they had the good fortune to know they couldn't do it, and they wouldn't do it because inside they knew they would just be creating what they are.

So we don't have to punish anyone because you are already having that experience. I am endeavoring to bring you out of the experience, just like Saint-Germain did at the dinner table and why he was such a wanted guest. You know, there was no woman that wanted to take him to bed and no man that wanted to take him to bed, because he was an original, secular consciousness. He was his own being. I mean, everyone knew he was unapproachable. Everyone knew that, because they knew that to be in his presence, they would have to be humble, they would have to listen, and they would have to want to know. And they all wanted to know what this man of magic knew. He was the ultimate, ultimate antagonist against Don Juan's reality. He was the ultimate creature who begged us to dream further than we had ever thought before.

So why? Because Saint-Germain was not an emotional man. I mean, he just didn't have any. He didn't have any. He didn't have any sex, victim and disease, power, tyranny, victimization. He didn't have any of that; you do. That is your modus operandi. So he could walk in your audience and be clearly his own being, and he would be a mystery and full of mystique and beautiful, and would have the ear of everyone sitting at the table. Why? Because everyone else is ordinary.

Now the miracle: Emotion was designed for us to experience what we had created in our mind. But we got so hung-up on feeling good, feeling bad, feeling rejected, feeling unworthy, feeling guilty, feeling lack, that we got into feeling; we couldn't even talk ourselves out of it. Well, then we are the body for disease. I mean, we really are. We are not preservable. I don't care. Don't give me any of that sympathy horse dung. We know our deepest sympathy. Our deepest sympathy is we made choices in this life. We chose to live by how we feel rather than what we know.

Now you know how many millions of years — look at me — you know how many incarnations you have lived and what you were looking at in the light? It is because, you see, an emotion is that you are in the middle of the experience and you haven't gained its wisdom; you haven't owned it. Ah, that is it. Now I can use this pebble as a stone to build a step, to build then another step, to build yet another step, and that is called evolution. Do you know how many millions of years you have reincarnated over the same emotions?

Why would the soul send you back? You think the soul sent you back to conquer what you don't know? No, it sent you back because you are in the middle — you are in the middle — of possession; you are in the middle of feeling.

You know the greatest truth you could say to someone? You could say this to them: "You know why you are important in my life? Because you make me feel a certain way. Do you know why I am changing and why you are not in the change? Because I don't want to feel anything because I want to create and have the space to experience the sensual actions from the fourth, fifth, sixth, and seventh seals. That is why you are not in my life, baby." Hard words? What, either you want it or you don't.

Do you know how many of you here are waiting, are waiting for someone that you can fall in love with that isn't even about their image, isn't even about their sexuality, isn't even about their past, so brand new, so clean? An amnesiac. Yeah, baby. Oh, God, bring me an amnesiac. Well, yes, it is a workable, plausible concept, isn't it?

Let me tell you. Let me tell you something. You are going to know it anyway because you are going to die if you don't understand what I am telling you; you are going to see it in the light. So how do we know we haven't already died and I am preaching to you in the light? I mean, how many chances do we get? How many halls of mirrors do we get to look into? Maybe we are already dead. Oh, lordy. Maybe we are already dead and we are having a light review.[6] However, now we can really put a twist on this. Maybe we haven't died

---

6 See *Ramtha, The Mystery of Birth and Death, Redefining the Self* (Yelm: JZK Publishing, a division of JZK, Inc., 2000), pp. 130-136.

but this moment will be in our light review, so we are going to die and we are looking at it, so we are reliving it, and we are hearing the same teaching. How many "Groundhog Days"[7] do we need? How many of them? How many light reviews, baby? How many of them?

I mean, maybe outside of this arena and outside of your house there is a curtain; you know, it is just a little tiny community but the little tiny community is all a prop. It is all a prop. Look around. We are all a prop. You know, I can take this on and really do a mind game with you. Oh, you like it? Well, let's say that then every time we are at an event, you go home, and you muddle around in your life and you change it, and every time you come to an event you have actually died and you are in a light review. What if I told you that? What, are you going to prove it otherwise? Because you are living in a dimension where you are still alive. Down here there is a grave marker for you — a grave marker. Maybe this is the big class in the sky. Maybe you are in the big class in the sky. I keep telling you it is an illusion. Don't believe me? It is a big class in the sky. Well, look at you, how slow you are to learn, how slow you are to give up to become.

You know, I used to tell my Dialogue group this. You know, they used to be with me two and a half days, three days. And, you know, they used to ask me, "What is the meat and potatoes of your teaching?" I mean, now — now — now you begin to see how many words have happened since those days, so now you see how I must handle the answer. And I would say, "Overcome and overcome and overcome till you become." It is still in effect today.

---

7 *Groundhog Day* (Bill Murray, Andie MacDowell: Columbia Pictures, 1993).

So is it possible you will be born as one of those really original beings, a man, a really original man, so enlightened, so pure, and so beautiful? His consciousness isn't in his first seal and he is really beautiful. And all the beautiful women try to rustle around him and try to be unique and outdo each other. I mean, he doesn't even see them because that is not what he is. That is not his fantasy. That is not his fantasy, and they haven't gotten the message yet.

Suddenly here comes this very ordinary-looking person who is reincarnated, is very ordinary but very mindful and very beautiful in their mind. And they fall madly in love — madly in love, mind to mind — mind to mind, and slowly a courtship — A courtship? Well, a courtship is the mindfulness that slowly gets to play down six seals into copulation, but it has to be in the seventh seal to start with. And it is how we make love do we make life.

Having children is a sacred act. Making love is a sacred act. I mean, it is all right if you are sixteen and you have just got problems. And don't ask me what they are because I may explain them to you. But don't pretend you are sixteen again, not in that mode. Grow up. Be mature. Be mature men and women. Start growing up.

You want to create the miraculous? Start in the first seal. Start there. This is really a class of masters, and it starts as crudely and as basic as today. But as basic as today, we begin to find and to delve into each one of your mystical minds what really lies behind your intent and what lies behind your children and what lies behind your barrenness. It becomes very obvious.

We also understand whose children you are. Why blame your parents? They had a fantasy, you were created, but you were equal to that creation. I mean, you are having the same fantasy.

It is the thing you did in your last life and you are facing in the light. You are going to come down to people that are doing the same thing. I mean, my God, do unto others as you would have them do unto you goes a long way. How many of you understand? Think unto others as you would have them think unto you. Think unto your children as you would have them be.

So now we have come really full circle from the most basic human need and human ignorance: sexuality, children, copulation, intimacy, the sacredness of the act or the crudeness of the act. And then we get to see why I am telling you take responsibility for your life. You are the one that came into your parents. And, yes, they had that fantasy, but guess what. Out of millions of spermatozoa, the fantasy that made the body was just right for you.

The Moral of the Story

So what does this have to do with relationships? Well, there are a lot of women in this audience and a lot of men in this audience that need to understand something: that to love another person means the unequivocal love of yourself. And loving of yourself isn't about buffing your fingernails and it is not about the hairdo that you have. It is not about the muscles you have or the breasts that you have or how many times you starve yourself so you can be thin. And I can tell you, you do that and you know that you do that. That is not about loving yourself. Wake up.

Loving yourself is living to your highest moral and spiritual aptitude. That is loving yourself. And to love another person is only equal to what you feel about yourself spiritually. Anyone can be a body. We can take everyone in this audience, young and old alike, give yourself to me for ninety days; if you want to make a body, I know how to make a body. Not only are you going to be buff, you are going to be analogical and you can do anything. I know how to use muscles. That is not what I am here for. I am not here for that, and you should be glad.

Now, masters, let me get back to this subject matter because it is important. If we spent as much time developing our great moral mind, if we spent as much time developing our spiritual self — not our carnal self; carnal selves come easy; spiritual selves don't because they are undeveloped — if we do that, then we can love someone. And then that someone doesn't have to be a someone that needs us so much in order for their life to continue. We can love someone and dedicate our precious temple, which the body is then; if God is made manifest, then the body becomes the holy temple. Then we can share the temple and ritual with someone that we love, clean and virtuous and honorably. That is all right. It is beautiful.

But if we are scoundrels, if we suffer from the psychosis of our image, we will never be faithful to anyone. Moreover, we will never be honest with anyone because we have never been that to ourselves, because if we had, we wouldn't be in a dishonest relationship. Are you listening?

If we had indeed revered ourselves and honored ourselves, if we understood that our semen — for men, because I was a man — that our semen was alive, men of virtue don't spill their seed unless it is in the name of love and sharing, and that could only be equal to who they are, who we are. We can love another because of the love we have for ourself. "I give you the gift of my seed. I have not spilt it through masturbation daily because I am in a habit of doing that. I have honored myself and treasured myself and loved myself. And when I give myself to you, it is truly a gift." That is a moral person.

Are there such people? Yes. Have there been such people? Yes, great people, great men and women. What are Christs? They know that the semen is alive and they know that it is energy, and if they do not spill it needlessly, they can use the energy right into their brain to focus on that which is termed perfecting the moral life.

Any master who wants to be a master does not have a debt, because that is the past and it is not the present. And when we forgive that who owes us, then we are freed up to live in the present, and that is more precious.

To the person we may forgive, they may think we are a fool. They may celebrate our kind heart, but they have just been released from their honor.

So what is a true master? One who is so present cannot occupy the space of the past and forgives those who owe them money. Now you begin to see why the lofty ideal up here has no commonplace practicality in life. But a Christ doesn't go after the practicality in life but to make known the spiritual image of God.

Kindly don't go to sleep. It is true; there are elder people in this school who have heard these words many times, but you have never been as evolved as you are this moment. And perhaps you begin to understand what I am telling you, that in the divine present, in the moment, this that I have taught you, this box that we see out of our frontal lobe, we want to clean it up. We do not want that only this much of our box right here,[8] this fine little center, is all that we have available for manifesting greatness.

Well, every day we have to keep renewing our past, our debts, our loves, our angers, our hatreds, our selfishness, our

8 The frontal lobe.

image, that it takes so much of the moment up. No wonder we are spiritually starved. The mind is starved. It takes a mindless person to keep it going. You know why? Because the mind is the phenomenon. The mind is the extraordinary. The mind is the emulous creature that creates reality.

CHAPTER 5
True Beauty and Originality

When Blasphemy Is the Name of True Conquest

So listen to me. Listen very carefully. I know I am touching hard and delicate places, but that is what I want to do.

Now I want you to know something; actually, I want you to know everything. Did you know that no one, except the great masters of antiquity and those who were public about the teachings, ever said that you too are a Christ — that was what was so outrageous — and that you are God? That was blasphemy. It is blasphemy in the West. It is blasphemy in the East. It is blasphemy in the North. And if you are truly going to conquer your image, it is real blasphemy in the South. I like it. Might as well be an original.

And so what did I care? What did I care? The same as Yeshua ben Joseph: I have a message and I am going to deliver the message. And the people who try to destroy it are destroying it because the message undermines the lifestyle that they have grown accustomed to living. And the message is: You are God. Don't you think it is time you acted like one?

Now what kind of impact does it have on your life? Well, to certain masters of antiquity, it cost them their life.

I tell you the most sublime and beautiful of men is a man who walks in grace, who is impeccable to his spiritual self, who loves himself not for the reflection in the mirror but for what comes out of his eyes, what is spoken from his lips, what he feels in the tears that he sheds. That is a beautiful man, a man who is not ashamed to accept back one hundred years everything that he has said, a man who is honest, a man who is not opportunistic, a man who uses his mind in the most brilliant of ways and understands that the most satisfying thing at the end of the day is not a roll in the hay but to how much were you able to influence your own life from a loftier perspective.

A great and beautiful woman is not a woman judged upon her face, her figure, like so many of you are involved in. That is not life. The natural biology of your life has given you a pleasant time in life to where you are the most beautiful and blushed with the opportunity to bear children. You have the figure; you have the breasts; you have the uterus; you have the face. That is only for a moment. That is only for the sake of capturing and copulating.

But true beauty is not to do with one's body. It is the originality of the Spirit, the dancing eyes and the mind that is quick, a Spirit that knows and understands challenges in life, that does not depend upon other people, does not depend upon another man, and does not spend her life trapping a man. A spiritual Christ that is female is truly an awesome thing to behold, and it is admirable and rarer than two moons in the sky.

This is an entity self-contained within their own power who falls in love with themselves. When you love yourself, you perfect the thoughts, you perfect the actions, you perfect the dreams, that suddenly the center of your nucleus is not someone else but yourself. The center of joy is not someone else but yourself and doing those things that bring to you at night a happiness and a sense of glee, that what you did was greater than your body, was greater than your genetics — it was greater than your gender — that at night you realize the great things that you lived for your day that transcended the relationships in your life, that made you wiser, more beautiful, and more spiritual.

When you develop the body, oftentimes you starve the mind. You starve the mind for the sake of bodies, your chemical reactions, because you are a bag of chemicals, you know. You starve that for the fulfillment, and you think that is living. But did it ever occur to you that maybe living is a higher order, a mind that is so sharp and so powerful it can manifest anything? Does that exclude the body? No, the body becomes the perfect temple of a great and masterful leader.

Does this mean you will never have sexual relationships again? No, but it means that they will be more cherished, more real, and more in the moment, and not artificial. Does it mean that you are going to miss out on business opportunities? No, it just will make you wiser, more clever, and more knowing. You will be light-years ahead of the game. Does it mean indeed that you have missed out on seeing the world? Once you have seen the world in only a microcosm of here and there, you will realize how ignorant the world really is. How many of you have understood what I have taught so far?

The Greatest Mystery of All: The Self

So, my beloved people, our study in the Ancient School of Wisdom was to study the greatest mystery of all: Who are we? And of course you can never address who we are unless you address that which is termed the intricacies of the biological system to which we call "we" and understand how it works. And of course then, though we can fully analyze it and dissect it and we can see it laugh and cry in life and we see it morbid and cold and stiff in death, we have to ask ourself where lies then the essence that gives it animation and then thereby is gone and has given us only that which is termed a stiff ember, a pitiful remembrance of the animation of life. What is it that gave it animation?

You are not your bodies; if you were, you would go to the grave. And when that undertaker sucks underneath your armpits and between your legs, starts pumping out all the blood of your body down into some sewer on that which is termed a cold, stainless steel gurney, can you really say then, "I was my body"? Because if you were, you are going down the gurney and you are going to the worm, and you are embalmed with chemicals that only preserve an image. But what was it, that delightful entity, that the body was the stage and all of the players that performed the play? Who was it that the body was performing the play for? It is that which has left the throne, and the players have no one to perform for anymore. That is what we call biological death.

So as much as you have heard about the body, simply to educate you that there is no molecule, there is no peptide, there is no hormone in the body that does not carry with it an intent, an information, and that the information is carried to every cell in the body[1] so that the cell can change costumes, and that we have to come back to this point then: Have we really been wrapped up in playing the part too long, have we really taken too seriously our costume, and have we rehearsed the lines too long? So who is the performance for? The entity that you have been practicing to be. And when you listened, who is listening to the voices? That is who you should be, who is listening, not the voices, because that is the eternal. That is the director of the entire escapade.

---

1 See Candace B. Pert, *Molecules of Emotion* (New York: Simon & Schuster Inc., 1997).

So what is a master then? A master is one who understands this and understands that the body is coagulated thought, indeed it is coagulated intent. And in its marvelous complexities, its marvelous operation, it is a tribute to who we were, not who we are. Who we are is to challenge who we were, to be who we are. Do you understand? How many of you understand?

The body lives in the past. Who we are is the present. We use the past and challenge the past to become the present. We use a past-coagulated thought from the present in which to exercise our intent. And it is our job to make the past molecule — the past biorhythm, biophysical, bioscience, bioectoplasm — of intent to be our will. And the reason we use it, it brings to the table experience and preparation. And what it lacks we will give to it in the form of will. Where it lacks courage, we will encourage. When we encourage, we change those molecular peptides.

Don't you ever think for one moment that amino acids are stable. They are not. And don't you ever think for one moment that there is some rudimentary law that every day that you wake up that you are pumped full of the same chemicals; you are not. Every one of those molecules are changelings. Every one of them can be changed with attitude and intent. Don't you think for one moment that your DNA is static. It is not. There is a whole lot in junk DNA you have never been and is the potential of becoming that was given to you by the Gods, your progenitors of the neocortex.

Don't you think for one moment that your body is static. It is as pliable as the caterpillar to the butterfly. Any molecule can change with intent because they are only handmaidens of intent.[2] The cells are getting the information. Don't you think for one moment that your cells have a static linear expression.

2 See Fig. G: Cellular Biology and the Thought Connection, p. 253.

149

They do not, unless you are dead already consciously; then they are going to follow the biological clock of the DNA in its life expression. And little will the environment ever affect it because the environment is only that which is termed the product of the Observer, and in this case the Observer has simply been emotion. And everyone agrees on that. That is why you have capitalism.

So a master doesn't have a face; only the players in the costume ball have a face. The master — the master — isn't here for pleasure, only the players in the drama reading their script. Only the actors have a script; the viewer doesn't. Are you with me?

So now why do the voices speak to your head? Why do the representatives of the collective body converge in the head and argue for attention? Because they are arguing through the throne of God for precedence, for equitably the continuity of their feelings. And what happens when the God is passive and allows it? Then all you are is the continuity of your emotions. That is all you are.

What happens one day, just like on the Plane of Bliss, when you already know you are doing a light review — you already know that — and you can change anything? What happens the day that you realize, that you stop playing the part and become that to which all parts plead for recognition? That is the Lord God of our being. That is what science can never, ever figure out. Science can only study the effect, can only study the phenomenon, can only study the quantum randomness of its expression but can never find the Source. The Source can never explain, be explained by, science; never will be. Never will be.

So when do you become the Observer? In the School of Ancient Wisdom students come to learn to be that, to learn to choose. And they understand that the choice is a great sacrifice because suddenly they are taken out of the spotlight as the drama actors and they are put in the role of the director. Does anyone really want to become what is faceless, what is not out there projected on the screen of quantum potentials? Not any image would want that.

So why are masters so rare? Because it takes a very rarefied being to say to themselves, I have got to be more than my senses. There is something more to me than eating, having sex, going to sleep, waking up, romance, integration into society. There has got to be more. And how do I know there is more? Because there is this big hole inside of me that no amount of money or food or sexuality can ever fill. It is a bottomless pit. It is what the Christians call the great Satan. It is a bottomless pit. How can I fill this up? By being it.

There is a part of us that knows that we are noble. So when do you select that? When you stop running these molecules and look at them for being the reason for existence, really and truly, when existence isn't about what you are going to eat, and it isn't about who you are going to seduce, and it isn't about another human being. It is about something that is much more extraordinary than any sensational touch that can be calibrated emotionally in the form of molecular looping to the brain and back to the body, the body back to the brain. You must be more than that.

The School of Ancient Wisdom that always brought about the greatest masters of antiquity are those who were ready to learn to be the Observer without the narcotic effect of emotions — and all emotions are a narcotic — to be that, to make a real clear choice. How many times have I been a man or a woman, and how many times have I had a sexual experience in ten and a half million years? How many bodies have I seen — how many breasts, how many vaginas, how many penises, how many muscles, how much hair, how much face have I seen — in ten and a half million years? How much longer can I duplicate that? When I say I really want to see the cosmos of the Milky Way, do I really mean that? I don't have an emotional hit on the Milky Way but I certainly do on my erection.

The day that you decide to be the Observer, whose dreams can reach the Milky Way, that that is what you want more than the erection, is the day that you will experience the Milky Way. It is the day that you will travel with Gods who really are very grown-up and very mature. The school is about understanding that the molecules of emotion work hand in hand with the progress of the soul and its intent on this plane to make known the unknown and to conquer what is the agitant in the soul, the agitation of an emotion. Look at that. You could be wearing today what you were never able to get over six million years ago. You could be wearing it today in emotions.

How do you get over it? Deciding to be that which doesn't feel anything chemically and to begin to encroach upon the sphere of knowing what it is. And with it comes that which is termed its own momentum of feeling, if you will, that has nothing to do with chemicals: God in its natural state of being — We who fell from Point Zero are the most jolliest of beings. We are the most beautiful of beings. We are without limitation. We are without fear. We are without lack. We are without unhappiness. We are the travelers of time. We have seen it all and done it all. And when we are thoroughly ourself, there is nobody, not even the body of Christ, can possibly magnify our brilliance. There is no molecule, there is no receptor site, indeed there is nothing that can give us what we already are naturally because God is love, and indeed "God is love" is the joy and the glue that holds everything together. The joy is in the glue, not in what is held together. Those are only choices.

And as we then make this journey, we can be assured of one thing: that no matter what comes our way in this life, we are worthy of that opportunity, and that we are equipped — not emotionally crippled but we are equipped — through the will, the scepter of decision, as to what we want. If we simply base every decision upon our emotions, we are doomed and we will never wear the crown of our God, of our Christ. We will never be boldly described as the traveler of time; we will only be another human being, who is never — Heroes: Heroes are the only thing that history ever remembers.

And what is the hero? Simply put, they are the ones that were the rogues against the system. That is why they were remembered. No one remembers all the "yes" people. Do they? No one. No one will ever remember you for being status quo. The only people that are ever remembered are those who listened to another drummer. They were out of step with all humanity. They are what is worth remembering. Shouldn't that be then a sign to you?

So travelers of time are those that have made marks in history. They were never the "yes" man or the "no" woman. They knew it and they did it and let everything fall where it was because they didn't do it for everyone's acceptance. They did it because they were compelled to do it, because they are travelers in time. They did not do it for emotion. If they had done it for emotion, they would never have done it. They would have been intimidated. Do you understand that? And they would never have made the choices they made because it would have cost them their marriage, their relationship. It would have cost them that which is termed their reputation. It would have cost them their gold. It would have cost them their privilege in society. If all of those were on the line and they still made the decision, then they put everything of emotion to the side and made the decision. Those are travelers in time. That is what the Observer is.

Now there are masters that are already in quantum time way beyond you, and you are still here groping about what your mother did to you. You are still fingering yourself with the abandonment of your father. You are still getting sick because no one loved you when you were a child. You are still throwing up at the thought of not being accepted. What kind of children are you going to bear? Neurosis; children who are prone to neurosis, psychosomatic-attitude behavior. That is what kind of children you are bearing. They are going to die early. Nature will take them out in the first plague. They are not equipped for it. They are not emotionally equipped for it. They are not biophysically equipped for it. Do you understand?

> To everlasting life as being the time-traveler,
> God I Am,
> the Observer
> of this blessed life.
> So be it.
> To life.

Great Men of Renown

So the men who have come to listen to that which is termed the teachings of an outrageous entity in a woman's body are obviously men of renown. And they are here to listen to truth. They are more than the sum total of that which is termed their first seal. They are vacillating closer to that which is termed the third and onto the fourth. It is just oftentimes you want to define men by their sexuality. You insist upon it, and they acquiesce. But don't you know that their heart is not where their first seal is? If it were, you would have kept them there a long time ago. So the men, as well as the women, are in a move, evolutionarily speaking.

And I want to say on behalf of my beautiful men in this audience that they do have a greater dream, and indeed that they do have a greater desire, and that their ideals for mateship are much loftier than what women give them credit for, for there is not a man in this audience that would not like for that which shares his bed with him and indeed his seed with him that would not be able to share equally, par, a mind that is both challenging, invigorating, and that which is termed a creative Spirit that knows no boundaries and that which, above all, loves God more than they. There is no man in this audience that would not want such a woman and indeed such a mate.

So the men that are here then should not be categorized with that which is termed those who are vulnerable only to hetaerae, because they have come here for another agenda as well, for equally their journey is a journey that is filled with terrors and threats and battles and wars and always the past. And perhaps for a man, the most important of all challenges is failure in the men's eyes around him.

If a man can become greater than the challenges of his counterparts, then he is unequaled. A man who holds his esteem equal to the eyes of the men around him has many equals. And if women wanted ordinary men, there is certainly a marketplace to get them.

So then who am I addressing tonight? The point is that it doesn't matter what gender we are. We should never ally ourself to our gender but to our God. And that then speaks of the student on the path of the great Great Work. There is no woman that should beg consideration in the face of masculine attempt. There is no woman here that should say that "I am less because I am a woman and thereby put the responsibility of my care into my male." If you do, you are not in the Great Work. And I daresay, as it were, there is no man here that should say that he is superior to any woman; that he is only equal to mind.

So what does it say about every one of you here? Every one of you here has an Observer. Every one of you are ultimately that. To diminish yourself is to be less than that. To diminish yourself is to become the frailty of your biological, emotional propensities. To be the Observer and to say "I am creating this" and then the next statement is "I am looking forward to the experience" — not that the next statement is "I am creating this but it doesn't feel good to me or it doesn't feel right to me" — I don't want to hear that. A master of the Great Work says, "I am creating. It isn't a matter of how I feel. I will get to that when I manifest it. Anything other than that is just layering the past to my future."

The Retreat is very much about coming down to peeling the onion back, to finding that part that makes us afraid or insecure or unequal or unchallenged or makes us great or ungreat. And if we are going to find the core of who we are, somewhere along the way we must appreciate our beautiful feminine beauty, but it cannot be the end-all to everything. And it is only temporary. Moreover, we cannot get stuck in our penises and our prowess as a lover. And we cannot think that our success is taking another woman away from another man. We cannot think that way. That is the way old satraps think, and they are all dead. Somewhere we must lay that aside and reach for something deeper. We have to go deeper, and we have to

156

find that voice that just observes quietly, unemotionally, and simply is in a state of Isness, that no matter what we put at its feet is not going to make it greater or less.

That is what these Retreats are about, is finding underneath the woman the Observer and being it, being it as boldly as you have been a woman in all your cleverness and in all your manipulation and in all your lies and in all your gearing down for entrapment. And indeed it is finding the Observer in the man who tries and pretends to be brave and strong and spiritual and the breadwinner and sexual. The truth is that really godly men don't enjoy their sexuality that much. They do it for the sake of competition. A truly godly man finds it not on the high end of approval in his physical existence. Anytime you find a man who has more passion for his thought and his creation than he does for his body, you have found a God, and they are rarer than two suns in the sky. That is the journey.

Now why do we say "when you are older and wiser"? Does it mean that physical age must come before wisdom? Usually that is the truth. Why? Because usually that which detracts has finally given way and no one is interested anymore. That is when all of those emotions can finally become wisdom. When nobody cares any longer is when you get really wise. Older-and-wiser is the golden hall of the Gods, but we can become that even when we are in the blush of youth.

This Retreat is about finding the Observer beyond physical sexuality and finding it in a place that it fulfills us utterly — utterly — and that, women, you don't have to play your games anymore. What would you do in a fortnight if you didn't do that? What if instead of making love you told the truth? What if in a fortnight you were really who you were, the Observer; what would happen? Would a lot of things change? Yes, I like it. It is called chaos. They fall away so that something can match to what has presented itself. So who would you be if you couldn't be a hetaera? Do you have the mind? Do you?

And about you men: Are you really brave and beautiful without your sexuality? And who are you? Who is with you in your life? That tells you who you are. Could you be that on your own? Could you be honest and truthful? Would you dare to be emotional? Would you dare to tell the truth? Would you dare to do that? In a fortnight if you did, many things would change. And of those of you who nothing would change, then blessed are you, because you already are living the life of righteousness.

And here is the point. We are talking about fabulous wealth that everyone wants. What stands in the way of that? Pretense, hypocrisy, cheating, lying, all of those things that are not the Observer at all. If the Observer can observe fabulous wealth, then how do we create it? Do we put a feminine spin on it or a masculine spin? How are we going to get our wealth? Are we going to get it through a man? Are we going to get it through fight and treachery? How do we get it? Because don't you understand, my beautiful people, that the day the past is over for you is the day that whatever the Observer creates is without the attachment of the past.

What miracle must come into your life but must dress down for your approval? Good point, isn't it, because consciousness and energy is always creating reality, even the emotional body. I want you to be able to create clearly. I want you to create whatever the Observer sees without any ulterior motive. Ulterior motives are the games that men and women play in the fields of God. The clearest, cleanest, fastest way to manifestation is to create without gender. Then it happens straightaway. How many of you understand that? So be it.

If this life were over tomorrow morning, you would go

to the light, and you would have a lightbody that looks similar to the one you have but much more beautiful and much more radiant. And if we were to review the lightbody, you wouldn't have a body that was either gender, because who is doing the viewing? That is who we want to be. Got that?

So tomorrow you are going to have a woman scientist[3] come and talk to you about emotions; appropriate for a woman to talk to you about. But I want you to remember something in the middle of this dissertation: This is a scientist's point of view. Moreover, it does not explain the great and true self; it only explains the body and its emotions. Got that? Some of you need a scientist to tell you what I have been telling you all along before you accept. Others of you don't need that. It is just knowledge. You add it to your knowledge bank.

There is a circle that even I cannot get into, that I can explain around and around and around. But there is a territory inside of the circle. There are no words in any language nor are there any symbols to be able to explain what is in the circle. It is sort of like the frontal lobe. It is called the quiet area in the brain. It cannot be explained other than it is just quiet. But that is where the seat of consciousness gives its wishes to.

Inside of this circle, I can talk around it and around it and around it — and no one is more gifted in strategy than I am — but there is a place I cannot go into, and that is the place that is necessary for the hierophant to say: I have taught you a discipline. The discipline is to teach you to go to the place that I cannot take you. And the place is — I cannot make you be the

---

3 Candace B. Pert, neuroscientist and research professor in the Department of Physiology and Biophysics at Georgetown University Medical Center in Washington, D.C. She was responsible for the discovery of the opiate receptor in 1972. Her book, *Molecules of Emotion,* presents the findings of her extensive research.

Observer nor can I make you hear your own thoughts because you are always busy listening to me. Therein you must enter the circle. The circle is for disciplines[4] and, from the disciplines, self-realization and indeed illumination. You are only going to be illuminated in your true self if you apply what I have taught you, and then you walk into the circle, into the center nuclei. When you sit in the nuclei, you will see all of your reality. And every discipline I have taught you takes you to that center point. If you do not do that, you will be forever riding the rim of teachings without the experience of truth. And I never came here to deliver teachings without experience. They are hand in hand. The only way you are ever going to grow is to take the teachings and apply them. Got that?

This little Retreat is about entering the circle that is quiet, that no one can explain to you. I have given you the disciplines. It will take you right into the nucleus. If you don't apply them and you don't go there, then you do not deserve the fruit of what the experience will yield to you. None of you do.

Now you want to be a God? I have taught you how to be a God. God is the Observer. How indeed can we be the Observer every moment of every day? You enter the circle and not be afraid to observe the thinking process of the carnal brain that you have created in this lifetime and the reality to which you have created. And at that same nucleus, from the Observer, the Observer has the power to spring forward and grasp any dream in its clutch and make it happen. But that dream can only happen if it is transcendent of one's past, because every day the dream of the image goes on and on and on and on. Got that?

---

4 Ramtha's disciplines of the Great Work are practical exercises that allow the student to experience the teachings firsthand. In this case the discipline is called "listening to the voices" and it is simply the act of quieting the body to become acutely aware and observe the continuous stream of thoughts we entertain in our head.

This is the gift of seven years on my rock. This was the gift of my pain. And this was the gift of what happened to me when I left the rock, for I was not the same creature that, wrecked and half-alive, was put there that descended. You are going to enter my rock, and you are going to learn the things that I learned that allowed me to be a changeling and allowed me to be the wind or this woman or that which is termed a sweet caress on your face or the kingdom of heaven. The Observer knows no boundaries. Got that?

Love Is a Many-Splendored Thing

Now where was I? I am going through my mental notepad here. I realize I have bored a lot of you and I have pressed a lot of you. When you are old — You have to understand this about old folks; they just ramble on and on and on.

So I want to talk about a couple more things because you are just ripe to hear them.

Well, I shall repeat that which is termed a seventeenth-century poet who said love is a many-splendored thing[5]. It really is. Love is a many-splendored thing.

---

5 We were only able to trace the phrase "Love is a many-splendored thing" as far back as the 1800s. This phrase was used in the 1955 film by the same name (Twentieth Century Fox: William Holden, Jennifer Jones). This movie was based on the book, *A Many-Splendored Thing* (Boston: Little, Brown and Company, 1952), an autobiography by Han Suyin, pseudonym of Elizabeth Chow Kuanghu Comber. Toward the conclusion of her book, Suyin cites the English poet Francis Thompson (1859-1907) and his poem, *In No Strange Land*, as her source:
"The angels keep their ancient places:
Turn but a stone and start a wing
'Tis ye, 'tis your estranged faces
That miss the many-splendored thing."

So what do you call love? I have watched many of you define love, but you don't even know what you are talking about. Listen to me. It is important that you learn. Love is not about the first seal, going to bed with someone, copulating with them. That is not love; that is lust. And many of you have lusted your way into responsibility of children, not even having the opportunity of having love as a many-splendored thing.

Now there are many of you in this room that have abusive relationships. Do you really think love is loving someone who abuses you because that is all you are worth? No, love is not abusive, love is not insecure, and love is not about lust. But true copulation comes in the midst of the blooming of love.

Love, lust, the need for companionship are all very different areas. The basic animal lusts for procreation. They don't know it in the moment but they are chemically — chemically — espoused to copulate, and the consequences of it are the next generation. You are very wise, some of you. You have learned how to avoid that nasty little aftereffect of lust. Some of you haven't. Some of you went after lust only to bear children, and you didn't give any consideration as to the aftereffect of it because what everyone, including myself, has a great and deep and profound longing for is love. It is a mystery. But once we find the mystery, it is a many-splendored thing. It is a phenomenon, and yet it is the basis of life itself because we are, in the greater view, loved into life. We are loved by a higher order that is so passionately involved with us that but for that passion, we would literally be nothing: with no memory, no past, no present, no future, no hope. We would be a nothing.

But something loved us into this life, loved us into animation, loved us into adventure. That is the first great love. And I can tell you, for one who reached the higher order of that love, it is a many-splendored thing. And it is, to the most primitive, a love that is the basest relationship to two people who are drawn together, who chemically are drawn together, emotionally are drawn together, because usually people, like animals, are not drawn together unless it is of a chemical nature. And the difference between friends and lovers is that lovers are the opposite sex. It is the only thing that a friend cannot share that a lover can. And there are some of you who have crossed all of those lines.

Now is it natural? It goes back to who are you and what is your prerogative in life. Everyone can make love. But everyone can make sex, but is sex necessarily love? It is not. It is convenience and it is chemical. Love is that lofty, golden existence that transcends the lust but, once it is found, includes it in the form of passionate oneness, a oneness that is shared not only sexually but is shared spiritually. It is shared in humanistic forms. It is shared in dreams. It is shared as not one leaning on the other but the two strong and able to walk and to define reality, and to be able to interlock those realities or keep them separate. But it is a companionship of greatness on every level.

And many of you in this audience are very wrapped up in clouding up this moment with that very problem of your nature that is so basic — so basic and so animal — that I would be even ashamed to be associated in the same category, because had I wanted to be a hare or a stallion or a mare or an ass or a dog, I could have been that. To be human — to be human — is to be simply the garment worn by the divine.

There is a lot of propaganda in the world about sexual freedom and about that that is the most essential thing in a relationship. I beg to differ. It is not. What is most important in a relationship is honesty, individuality, greatness in its own uniqueness because that is what is everlasting. This is a society of decadence, and if you don't already know it by now, you too are a fool again. How many times tonight have you been that? And the only thing that separates you from the animals in the forest is that you control — you control — the weapons that control them. That is the only thing that separates you.

Now love is a many-splendored thing. And it is not something that starts between our legs. It is something that starts in our soul and only there. It is something that allows, as the most perfect, polished mirror — of either the copper of an early morning or the quicksilver of a waxing moon — a mirror, a reflection of ourself. The splendor is to be able to interact in a mirror of a perfect reflection, and that when we look in that mirror and if we find that reflection beautiful, satisfying, challenging, exciting, if we fall in love with the reflection that in its eyes hold a promise of new unfoldment, of new adventure, of new awareness, if we look into the mirror and that when we touch the mirror, the reflection comes up to meet our touch, and if we move our finger, the mirror moves with us; if we turn around, it turns around, but only to look back to make sure we are looking — Love is a many-splendored thing. Whether the mirror is copper, silver, whether the mirror is quicksilver or midnight blue, it has a reflection.

And the reflection of love as a many-splendored thing is essentially the reflection of ourself, and that when we look in this mirror, we are looking at another entity. But the entity spontaneously puts up its reflection that we meet it on the mirror, that it smiles and we smile, that its eyes dance and our eyes dance, and that when we come together, full body, and we touch, the only thing that separates us is that it is an illusion of our own reflection. Then we are in splendor.

What does this mean? A reflection in the mirror will never

be dishonest. A reflection in the mirror will never lie. A reflection in the mirror will never animate on its own. When we look at the reflection, it looks at us squarely. And even when we turn our backs to glance to see if it is still there, it is looking back at us. It has no past and it has no future. It is our partner in the moment of our delight, in the moment that we celebrate some primeval, celestial place.

When we love what we see, we do not copulate the mirror. We do not rape the mirror. We do not abuse the mirror. We are fascinated by it. That is splendid. And when we have someone who we begin to question are they the mirror or am I, when it is that close we have found love, because in that we have found our delight, our nakedness, our glory, our beauty, our happiness.

You have confused the issue about what a relationship should be. It should never be based on sexuality. If that is all it is, it should be made clear that this is but a chemical moment and nothing more lies beyond it. And if you find then that you are addicted to the chemical moment, then that is the sum total of the reflection, that when you look in the mirror you will always pull your pants down and look at your rear and look at the only place that matters, and you will never see the full reflection. That is just simply the way it is.

Too many of you love people for the way they look and are utterly dissatisfied with the way that they are. Then that is your delusion. There are many of you who find each other happy in bed as willing partners, and in that moment everything is possible, right before orgasm. But when orgasm is finished, is everything still possible? Rarely, because when you only love people for their sexuality, then you are a fool and so are they.

To love another person is to love us like we see ourself in the mirror and not some body part to facilitate our body part.

A master would never do that. And if they ever did, it was a part of the past that they have cleaned up and left no footsteps.

And love is a many-splendored thing. And the greatest love is that essence about a person that moves us — moves us — in a way we have never been moved before, who haunts our mind, who is our ideal. It is a person that no matter how much we embrace and how deep we go, we can never find the end of them. And it seems as if we want to be lost in them and that their moment is our moment, and that when we are apart, the splendor of that euphoric coming together is always there. We truly have found a mate on the highest level of ourself. Now that is love.

And the reflection brings out the greatest in us, not the least in us. The reflection calls upon us to be our most beautiful, our most polished, and our most refined, not our most decadent, our less, our weakness, our fear. You never look in the mirror to see that. You look in the mirror to see yourself.

So many of you here go to your lowest denominator and call that love. And if you are masters in the Great Work, you should be masters in every part of your life. And this is a holy thing, this body. It is not for sale. A God lives in here. It shouldn't be trashed for the sake of orgasm, that it should be kept somehow sanctified for something truly wonderful. Don't go around looking to be laid just because you are horny. Go around; change your perspective. Look and see if you can see your reflection in a madding crowd. And maybe that reflection won't look like anything you thought it should look like, but maybe its essence, its magic, its — You can take the most beautiful woman you think in the world; if she doesn't have essence, she has nothing. You can take the youngest, most virile man in the world, but if he doesn't have Spirit, he soon is nothing. It is about that which is our reflection. That is what we should love.

166

There are many of you here that are holding onto people, that the only time that you ever meet is in bed, but the rest of the day you are at odds with one another. That is not love. That is sexual dependency. And when you don't recognize it as love, you live out of guilt and responsibility, only waiting for that next moment to where you copulate because that is the only point that the two of you come together in agreement. Everything else is disagreement. You do not do that to a mirror. You do not do that to your reflection. And yet your unhappiness, your anger, your abusiveness comes from the total lack of growing in something, that the only way that you have communication with it is through sexuality, and your growth is stifled.

You hate the person but you love the person. You love to hate them. You love to make them miserable. You love to find fault in them. You love to find lack in them. You are a busybody. You are a gossip. But they got your number, because the only way that you kiss and make up is in bed, and it is not in life at all. That is not a relationship based on love. That is not love that is a many-splendored thing. That is a relationship born out of guilt and sexual need. That is in error. All of you have done it. You don't have to do it again.

If you are abusing the person you are with, you are beating up on them because you can't beat up on yourself. You are in lack, you are ugly, you are trapped, you are miserable, and you then cannot break away because that is where you have your link.

So love is not just in bed. It is early in the morning. It is in the splendor of the noon. It is in the sleepiness of the afternoon. It is in the golden hour. It is sharing the silent whispers of light in the golden hour. It is everything.

Women, you live with your men because you know how to get a man in bed and you know what to use to get them there. But you think that is going to keep them there? You are a fool — you are a fool — because if the only way you can get a man is through your sexuality, then I can guarantee you one thing: There will be other women much cleverer than you that will come along and use the same tools. Now we have got a problem, and the problem is infidelity. So he is seeing someone else and you thought that he loved you. He didn't love you. You accommodated him and you used it to trap him. What else do you expect from the relationship?

There is always going to be someone better than you. Don't you know that, or are you living in a dream world? And if that is the basis of your relationship, then you really don't love yourself; I can tell you that. You abuse the tools of your trade that are as old as the foundations of the world. And you have gone no further than that, no further than development, and all you are worried about is keeping him in line: He doesn't look at another woman, he doesn't go to bed with another woman, that he brings home the paycheck, that he is faithful to you. What do you have to offer? And, moreover, what kind of man have you got trapped here? Maybe he is not worth — maybe he is not worth — any of it. That is not love is a many-splendored thing. That is a trap of many-splendored ways.

Are you wise? Are you thoughtful? Are you wise, are you thoughtful, or are you just clever and pretty? And are you trying to get pregnant so you can cement the relationship? You know, who are you? What is your agenda? Your children are going to grow up and leave you one day — don't you know that? — just like the man that you trapped. He is going to leave you too. What have you done?

You haven't danced with the image in the mirror, and you haven't loved it. There are beautiful women everywhere. You are not unique. What makes you unique — what makes you unique — is when you understand what I am telling you here: There is more to you than your body, and when that becomes the higher order of your existence, then you become unique.

And, men, why are you in this relationship? Are you in this relationship because she turns you on sexually but the rest of the time in your life she is a mess? How much of your life are you going to sacrifice just for copulation? Is that worth it, or are you afraid someone else will get her? Well, don't you know they are going to get the same mess you just had? Don't you want to share it? What is the problem here? Spread the mess around.

If you are there because it is sexual, then don't try to pretend it is anything other than that because she will always disappoint you and, furthermore, you will always disappoint yourself because that is not the basis of the union. How do we know that? Try being abstinent in your relationship for sixty days and see how that relationship has continued.

Is this man a meal ticket to you? Is this woman a prize? Is she really? If she is a prize, then every moment of your day is a basis for union. And if one of you is beating up on the other, it is because you are such a weak, backward, ignorant, jealous entity that you can't get on with your life and make a change from your sexual orientation in this partnership. You don't even deserve to have a new partnership. That is who you are. If you realize that, then you understand there is nothing here. My beating of this person is my sexual frustration in action. That is all it is. It is mindless. How many of you understand that?

What, are you trying to manifest a man because he is going to be wealthy and take care of you for the rest of your life? What happened to you? Are you saving your brains and body to manipulate him so he will bring home the paycheck? Is that what you are doing?

And what about you? Are you working all day to bring home the paycheck just so that you will get somebody to go to bed at night? You could have a lot less complicated relationships with sidewalk hostesses who only demand of you a few dollars but without the emotional problems that go along with it.

Now I don't want you to feel guilty about being in your relationship if it is for that. Why don't you just say that is what it is? That would be impeccable. That would be masterlike. Don't string another person on because you are just using them. And don't tell somebody you love them when you don't. The greatest answer to that is "I don't know what I feel for you because I don't know what I feel for myself. And if I am using you and the only way that you are possible in my life is in bed, then I don't call that love. I don't call it love for myself or for you. I would be lying if I said otherwise and that, even though I am a wretched soul, goes at least against some grain of my own interior morality."

Now no one in this room should live like an animal. There are very clever women in this audience that know how to use their bodies to get what they want, but unfortunately you will wear the yoke of their desire for a price. There are men in this audience that know how to lie to women and manipulate them for their bodies and never fully intend to live up to their very small-minded dreams. You shouldn't do that; none of you should.

Impeccability starts even when you are young. And love is a many-splendored thing. It takes a righteous life to find such love. It takes a righteous, moral life to find such love. It takes an entity not willing to sell their body or their soul for any kind of comfort. It takes an entity who loves their soul and their Spirit and the body that they inhabit, that they find pure unto their own eyes. They may be laughed at by the whole world, but there are other masters in the world that are on a great path that feel the same way.

Now I know that I have taught you from the place to be God and to manifest your life. You can do anything you want to do. But I will tell you that these things that are stigmas to you, that make you like elephants in quicksand, this is one of your weaknesses and it shouldn't be — it should be one of your strengths — and that to have the greatest relationship in this school is to have one not based on popularity, not based on physicality, but based upon setting all of the garbage aside: all of the lovers, all of the women, and all of the men, and pushing them aside even though your habit is screaming for companionship.

Learn to be the dancer in the mirror, do, practice it, learn to be that. You are not going to know the difference to was it the mirror that raised its hand, or did I? Did I raise my hand and it was merely my reflection, or am I the reflection of the mirror? And if you do that, you will find integrity in all seven seals. You will find purity in all seven seals. You will find honesty. And when you do that, you can't help but love who you are. And there may not be anyone in this school that appreciates you. It is not for them. It is for you. It is for you.

So what separates common beauty from uniqueness? Strength, tenacity, originality in thought, a woman who is her own power, her own genius; a man who is his own moral guardian; a man who doesn't live in the past, whose integrity is not about spilling his seed to prove his manhood but dared to dream concepts of thought that are fantastic.

There may not be anyone in this school for you. That is because you should be it for yourself. Beauty cannot be seen any more than love can. It is a state of existence that goes back now again to the spiritual in us. I am talking about spiritual attributes, the character, the wine that fills the glass versus just the glass.

I want all of you to know the kind of love I am talking about, but you are never going to know it until you face who you are. And there are some of you in this audience that have had long marriages, that the passion, long-gone, went out. The love of many-splendored things, long-gone, was covered up by responsibilities and problems and families and differences of opinions and friends and money issues and all of those sorts of things. Your job is to unpeel it all and find what drew you together in the first place and rediscover that love so sublime, so beautiful, so pure, and so clean, because anyone can worry but not everyone gets to love and be loved.

Now, my beloved people, how many of you begrudgingly learned something tonight? You did? You did? Do you suppose then that the teaching in its greatest effect — that the teaching tonight, no matter how graphic, how poetic, how simple, how challenging — could the teaching tonight have led you to a loftier, more self-caring or self-respective life, all the way to a life that we memorialized one Easter Sunday on a stormy morning, we celebrated the life of a great being?

Virtue is a hard road in some senses but it is worth it. Virtue — virtue — is honesty. Virtue is clarity. It is not using anyone. It is not lying to anyone. It is about being true to yourself. All of your guilt that you have harbored inside — and of all of the things you have done, of all the abuses that you have done to other people — are seeds for disease, and ultimately you will be at the hands of your own undoing.

The day that we open up and breathe very clearly and forgive our debtors, forgive those who have transgressed against us — Forgiving is not reembracing; forgiving is simply removing them from the aspect of our view that belonged to the past. And when we forgive, we allow the past to rest and to no longer occupy those precious moments that we have that beg us to renew our life and to become a new person, to reinvent, to give birth to ourself in a way that no one ever allowed us to do before.

Freedom and virtue are the same thing. They come at the cost and the willingness of that which shall enjoy that privilege: the hard work of forgiving your enemies and letting the dog die, clearing your window, forgiving your transgressors, forgiving the view that you accepted early in your life that led you to such troubled waters, to go all the way to the root of it and to forgive it and to be clean of it, and to entertain no one else in our life that reminds us of the lessness of ourself.

It is a terrible thing, people, when we go looking for trouble. It is a terrible thing when we go dig up our past because ultimately we are the hangman and the hanged. I will be happy, very happy, when all of you learn to reinvent yourself and not to become the lie of the past but who you want to be, full-bore, and to love yourself so much that you will never be abused by anyone again and never feel that you deserved it, ever, and to know and to have a quest for: I want to know love as a many-splendored thing. I can be an animal but I was born a man, and I was born a woman. I want to know the quality of myself. I want to know that and to be able to go after it, and to live it impeccably and not to breed like breeding stock for the sake of the next generation but to bear children out of a union that is that beautiful — that beautiful, that clean, and that pure — to trap no one only to fail to live up to what is expected of you outside of the bed.

So much to learn, and yet it is worth it because you get immortal life. You live long; you have pleasant thoughts and deep ones and they are not tainted with prejudice. They are not tainted with guilt and shame and ignorance. They are clean, like little children.

Christ said only until you become one of these can you enter the kingdom of heaven, and that is nearly the abolishment of the animal to the fairylike existence of pure God, pure youth, pure clarity without prejudice. And you are never too old to wake up to be young again. And you are never so bad that you cannot wake up and reinvent and be virtuous.

So now it is important, this talk to you. And, yes, you could say, "I could have figured these things out," but we would have had a much more progressive audience had we been able to do that. I have told you a lot of things tonight, that if you are really wise, young or old, you would think about and make some choices on. To cherish oneself — cherish it — have you ever thought about cherishing yourself? A unique concept. And love? Well, if you are really fortunate and you deserve it, you will find a dancer in your life, in the mirror, who will dance with you, and you will not know — you will not know — whether it is you looking at a reflection or that you yourself are but one. So be it.

So it is all right to make love but only when there is love.

FINALE
The Elixir: A Love in You Loving You

The elusive trance state is the key. It is the secret and the prize that is hardly ever recognized. Unfortunately, it is little understood and those who claim to know and theorize about it are often responsible for turning it into some unreachable, esoteric, shrouded-in-mystery, occult concept that strikes people with fear and concern.

The trance is a state more common in our experience than we realize it. It is nothing to be afraid of or assume that it is synonymous with witchcraft or quackery. For example, it is what people from every walk of life and culture at one time or another experience when they fall in love. They become transfixed in their mind with the thought of another person, a fantasy, a dream that uplifts and makes life meaningful. They call it *being* in love.

All of the wealth of imagery that has been used to describe love in song and poetry — images of being lifted, the sensation of floating, flying without wings, a sense of timelessness or time standing still, indescribable beauty, colors becoming alive and fluid, unearthly light, unlimited vitality, expansiveness and instant knowingness, clarity, peace, joy, inexhaustible inner strength, communion with extraordinary beings, banishment of borders and limitations, et cetera — all of these things are really describing the state of the trance, which love is. It is a dynamic state of creativeness from where new expressions of life flourish and evolve life everywhere. In this acute altered state of awareness, options are never stagnant, and challenges and limitations are not too great to overcome. Nothing seems impossible or unreachable in this presence of mind and self-identity. But when the vision is lost, the trance state is also lost, as well as the lofty vision in which we held ourselves. Love has withered and died.

Thus we see that the trance state and who we think we really are are intimately connected and reciprocate each other in a way that is not commonly perceived. That is why Ramtha continually says: "To fall in love with a person, another human being, has got to be the direct result of first falling in love with you."[1]

There is definitely a whole cascade of emotions and chemistry in the body associated with the experience of falling in love, but we must be careful not to confuse the true elixir with the effects of chemical emotions of action/reaction screaming loudly for attention in our heads: "So instead of wearing a crown of a thousand thorns we have but one voice, and one voice is that voice that is love that has brought us to this unifying moment in our life."

"I know these things," Ramtha declares. "And I know all of the potential you haven't used, and I know more than anything the one thing that you need and want more desperately than anything in your life, and that is to know that elixir called love that gives us a vitality — that gives to us, doesn't take from us — that gives to us that immortal joy and peace of mind that allows us to have one voice in our head instead of fifty voices in our head. And love does that."[2]

Love, when considered carefully, is *not an emotion* but the source of personal events that we then experience emotionally.

---

1 *Finding Peace in Love,* Tape 478 ed.
2 Ibid.

This is of the utmost importance to remember in our quest to understand this mystery. It is a subtle state of being that colors the world around us and is the springboard of our experiences, independent of who is in our lives or what possessions we have. The target for our love comes first into focus; then the journey called life follows. It is no different from Socrates' idea of "the good" — however subjectively defined — as the ultimate source and goal of happiness and platonic love. As Ramtha explains clearly, it is "the cosmic glue that holds everything together."[3]

Love is so precious and is called a divine elixir because it is the unique reflection of ourselves that defines us as eternal beings who cannot be defined in terms of random chemistry or physical emotion. As we have considered throughout this book, we are blatantly the players and the source who determine life's outcome and expression. Because of love we know we are divine beings. And just as love transcends all borders of physical reality, so is it our true nature and identity to survive beyond death and have the power to reach beyond the borders of space and time. It is against this framework that we can begin to entertain the possibility and the mechanics of the old concept of reincarnation or, if you prefer, the idea of life after death: "Love allowed this explorative consciousness to happen. But unfortunately a few emotional events and it gets cast into stone, and then everybody stops growing and then we have reincarnation because we wear out the bodies, but the lessons are unfulfilled."[4]

There is no hidden, esoteric mystery to reincarnation, as Ramtha explains, that "you are just an ongoing drama machine and you change more costumes than are in a Shakespearean play. You burn out bodies, but the mind goes on."

---

3 *The Emotional Body,* Tape 9428.1 ed. (Yelm: Ramtha Dialogues, 1994).
4 *Finding Peace in Love,* Tape 478 ed.

"Mind does not die. Mind never passes away. All reincarnation is is the need to keep picking up lives that we can burn out, hoping to get to a conclusion of wisdom."[5]

So we have now a greater picture of what this elixir called love is really about. It is the invisible that keeps our hearts beating and life flourishing and growing everywhere. It is the platform and the stage that allows the drama of our life to exist and be played out. It is a love in you, loving you into life. It is the enthralling vision that mirrors to us an abundance of reasons why to be alive. It is the magic wine on the lips and minds of Gods and Goddesses that inspire those mortals whose journey of self-discovery has just begun.

And the voice of wisdom gained through a remarkable life speaks across the oceans of time: "You all want love, the great fountain, the great elixir. It is true, to have that magic moment we would lay down our lives for lifetimes to relive it but for an hour. It is that great of a high, and it is that quintessential of an orgasm." But remember the Master's advice: "To love ourself is the beginning of the quest."[6]

— *Jaime Leal-Anaya*
Writer and Editor, JZK Publishing

---

5 *Finding Peace in Love,* Tape 478 ed.
6 Ibid.

CHAPTER 6
Impact on Reincarnation

Truth in the End Reigns Supreme

You have to ask yourself a really important question at this point. "My Teacher," you would think, "is teaching me about love." Well, I think I know about it; do you? Are you still with that first person you said you were madly in love with? Well, then we got to boil it down to its basic substance, that what you really did is that you had sexual love with them, and to this date very few of you have ever told that person the truth. You have not said to them, "You know what? I lied to you when I said I was in love with you. The fact of the matter is I wanted to have sex with you. I wanted you to have sex with me."

You haven't told them the truth, because they still think that you love them. And you are doomed to meet them in your next incarnation because of that, because you are going to have to tell them the truth because, you see, what was the basis of my teaching here? To make known the unknown and that through consciousness and energy we create a paradigm, we create it in mass, by collapsing particles into coagulated atomic structures in which we get to walk through with our emotional body to sensually experience that which we have created and, once we have done, to log back in the brain the experience. That shuts off the emotional body from continually wanting. We have used everything properly. We have used everything properly.

So these little amours of yours are going to be met in the next life. And as subtle and as casual as it is, your words are law, so you are going to meet those people again, and if you don't tell them the truth now, you are going to be reincarnated with them in which this scenario is going to happen again.

Truth leads us to love.

So you know you are on Earth and you say, "But, you know, the consciousness is free love now; nobody really means what they say." Tell that to a broken heart. And that is exactly what I am asking you to do.

So we find that there are animals higher than us. We find animals — animals — we find animals greater than us that can love forever. We find a worm can turn into a butterfly, can take their body and make wings. I always said that nature was beyond human consciousness, and it absolutely is. So you can beg off to your youth — you can beg off — but my question is to you: Why are you still having the fantasies?

So now we see that sexual love is about heat. We find that the second seal is about crippling love, crippling love. This love doesn't look for sex; it is looking for compassion and attention, which it thinks should follow sexual love. Now you have raised your hands and you said, "Listen, I absolutely felt bad so I could get some attention. I know I can make love. I know I can do that, but is that all that I am? And is this person I am with, is this all that I think about them? Because the only reason I think about them is when I am thinking about what I am going to do to them in bed and, quite frankly, the last few times I have been fantasizing about other things and other people. This has just become a body part for my mind to overlay to it."

This is heavy stuff. That is heavy stuff. In the name of love we have become hypocrites. We have become defilers. Instead

184

of being stoic, instead of being abstinence, no, we are going to get down there, but in the freedom of our quiet mind we will think about somebody else. And that is not a master. You know what? An eagle doesn't do that, absolutely doesn't. A butterfly only became one because the only conscious thought to the worm after its feast was to go to sleep and to change. I don't see that and neither will you in the world. This is what becomes disenchanting. And the world says they love this and they love that. They don't love that; they are in lust for it. So now we see that disease is actually created by the lack of love in which we have misinterpreted as attentiveness and allegiance.

And now we go to the third seal, which is power and victimization. And here we find the birth of gurus, priests, ministers, politicians, corporate internationalists, health gurus, beauty gurus — we find all of the people that have arrived — and through their certain knowledge gather people together and teach them how to be the status quo and feed off of them. They live off of them; they live. These kind of people can never retire, because if they retire they have no sustenance. And what is the love to a tyrant? Adulation, devotion. Devotion is the mother of ignorance. We have adulation, we have devotion, we have giving our power away because this is the big kahuna, this is the big lover, this is the big deliverer. "This is the person that is going to deliver my disease, that is going to get me over my heartache." I mean, they are out there by the millions. Anyone who wants to be anyone knows that. They are savvy. All they have to do is be an "enrioter."

Well, the third seal is when we bring in creed, religion, nationality, sexual differentials, politics. We bring in it all, gurus, you name it, because these people you vacillate to because they are the ultimate love, love parent in your life. People love their political candidate. People love their queen, their king.

What do these parasites do? I mean, they don't do anything to help the old people and the sick people. They take their money from them and live like queens and kings. But the poor starving wretch in the street is a royalist. Why? Hey, why are they royalists? Because even if they have no food to eat, they will sing *God Save the Queen*, not God save me but God save the queen. Give her another hat. I mean, and how about — hey, I am just getting started here; you ought to stay tuned — how about all those de facto princes and queens? You know, they wear all these medals. I mean, they are just glistening, you know. I mean, not one of those medals was to die for another person. Not one of them fought in a war to deliver their people from evil. Not one of them was to give unilaterally a disbursement of goods to all people and to give all people the royalistic doctor for good health, to give all children the right to knowledge as the prince or queen or king or princess has been taught. And they wear these medals? Where did they come from? I think they came from Cartier and Fabergé. That is my opinion of course. Those are not medals of honor; they are jewelry. There is not one king or ruling queen or ruling family that has ever dispatched of their royal household and lived in the hovel of their lowest subject, and if they did, they would deserve a medal.

Why do they do it? Because as wretched as they are, they are the people that belong to the Crown. They belong; someone needs them. They will give everything they have to support a decadent royalist regime so that all of the princes and princesses and duchesses and dukes, or whatever they are called, can drive around and play polo all day. They will give it to them and applaud them and work very hard to give eighty percent of what they make to these people that eat caviar by the pounds. And why? Because their leaders love them because they are the leaders of them, and without them there are no leaders.

Now we come to gurus, politicians. Gurus are charismatic leaders that just to be in their presence is the same thing as a subject in the presence of a king or a queen; it is just it is now called guru instead of queen or king. And that king or queen can do nothing wrong because this person looks at them as the ideal, the goodness of their life that they support. So is a guru. And we fall in love with power and influence, fame, fame. Well, if the latest famous person is double-aught size in their clothes, then that is the way everybody should be, because they are our new leader that we must follow, and if we follow them, we will be loved just as we love them.

Rap stars are a message of savagery and degeneration, but they are worshiped because they are degenerate and savage. But no one understands they do it just to make money and to make fame, to buy more cocaine and to buy more drugs and promote it upon their constituency.

So truth finally reigns supreme. Time preserves us as we are preserved in history. And if you have any ideas of having power over a constituency, you better think twice about what you teach them, because if you teach them so that they can accelerate to your approval, this is what is called hypocritical love on the third seal, the most powerful love there is.

Let me tell you something: There have been Republicans and Democrats that have been in love with their respective parties longer than their first sexual encounter. There are royalists who are in love with their king and queen and royal family and have more passion towards them than they did their first and second marriages. There are gurus that people follow that love the guru much more passionately than they have ever loved anyone they have said "I love you" to. Now we are talking about an orgasm. We are talking about this in power and what creates a royal dynastic family, what creates a despotic government, what creates leaders, what creates religious gurus, what creates famous people that are brainless but because they wear double-aught clothes and are thirteen years old they are somehow the saviors of humanity. Everybody gives their power away to them, and corporations expect for you to do that, because if they can hire them and set a precedent, they are the ones that have the product to sell you.

That is powerful. Look at me. You have bought into your personal society longer than you bought into your first "I love you." That is how powerful the third seal is.

I have more to say. We are going to make this a memorable teaching. So, masters, let us review what I have said. We all now understand sexual love is only as long as animalistic heat exists and then we are off to another session without any kind of remorse, without any kind of consideration. We simply don't feel the things we felt for that person. Well, if all that we feel for any person and that we have sold our soul to get what we want, then they are nothing but trash in our lives, and we ourselves are nothing but rolling tumbleweeds in the wind. We have found that we act like animals, with the exception of that there are animals in the kingdom of nature that are higher and more organized, more knowledgeable, more precise, and more decisive than we ourselves are. What a humiliating experience. But that is the truth.

We come then from sexual love, as long as the heat is on, to second-seal-attention/need love. We would go to any extremes to make people feel for us, to make them pay for their indifference, to make ourselves such a burden of compassion that we organize our lives absolutely around our own illness and the richness that it gives to us, not understanding and not willing to understand the consequences of this decision in long-term life, genetic life based in absolute decisive mind and emotion. But we will — we, you; I have my own story — you will do whatever it takes to get sympathy, compassion, and attention to the risk of your own physical health and well-being. And when that wears off we do not realize — you do not realize the consequences of trying to hold a fickle lover who is nothing more than sexual heat in your life, the long-term consequences of mental health and physical health. That shows the power, drawn like moth to a flame, of the magic power of love. And all along, all along, it has been hypocritical. It has been a decision made to the consequences of your own health.

And then we come to the third seal, a graduation, a moxie mind, a smartness upon human nature and what people need, and to be able to position ourselves in a full range from the king — in a social gathering of friends and neighbors you have got to be the one getting the most attention — to a neighborhood, to a town in social politics, to a county and county politics, getting the most attention, making the most promises, giving the most "I love you" to everyone just to get your vote and then "I am going to leave you after I have you," all of the way to state and national vote. It is the same thing. The first seal sets the pace of the other two seals involved in the three-seal triad of human nature.

All politicians are first-seal lovers on a mass. All kings, queens, nobilities, they are second-seal lovers occupying the third place. All personal tyrants have the same trickle-down effect in your own personal life.

Now love: Did any of this group — from guru, president, queen and king, to former lover, and in between disease and discontent and sorrow — did any of these people have love, or did they have the instinct to survive? Would you turn to your neighbor and answer the question. I just want to make sure we have got that in vocal record from you. The old lovers are not present tonight but the old actions are. How many of you heard what I just said? The old lovers are not present tonight but the old actions are.

Love then seems to absolutely escape priests, ministers — at least according to my teachings — kings, queens, duchess and dukedoms, and prime ministers and Republicans and Democrats and presidents and Muslims and Jews and Christians and atheists and dictatorships. When we take a look at all of them, did any of them ever show any love? So how much aligned are you to the pattern of your social-conscious group that you belong to? I want you to ask yourself this question.

Why did your parents love God? Because they were scared of him. They stopped living because they were afraid of him. He was — he — was the giver of life, but they refused to live life because they were scared of the giver of life who taketh. That is a powerful — that is a powerful — medicine in the hands of religion and governments and politics.

It is a new day, and it was a new day when I came here and I started with a handful of people. It was a new day when the message of Christ took on not a surrealistic meaning but a true and profound meaning of absolutely belonging, and not adoration but being an integral part of the life of love and the gift of love.

If God is love — if God is love — then we would not have the dissension of man over man or woman over woman. If God is love, then we would be in accord with the statutes of nature in its thrust to evolve. Nature is very cruel; it is the survival of the fittest. But just because a female eagle refuses to mate because the love of her life has been murdered doesn't mean that she will not survive, because that which she is guarantees that the fewness of her breed shows the rarity and the delightfulness of her character amongst the hordes of that which is termed the plains animals that are vegetarians and eat and eat and eat and eat and mate and mate and mate without any family unity nor without any need to love. Let me tell you, it would only take four wildebeests to kill a lion attacking a member of its clan, but they never do that. They run away in fright and let the lions murder their daughter, their son, their husband, their wife, their grandmother; they take them down. Horrible. It is horrible, and everyone who sees it should wince.

But you attack an eagle and his mate will come to the rescue, and you have to battle two and not one. No lion gives a damn about any of his cubs in his pride. If one of their jaws is broke by a zebra stud, they don't give a damn; they will let them die. I don't call that noble and I don't call that love, but you call it love because it is sexual. You have a dominant man; what do you need a dominant man for if he will not even stand up for you, take care of you when you are sick, and hopefully that you have enough love and enough compassion that you never get sick because you are filled with completeness in your life, and the only thing you have to worry about is people trying to destroy you.

So I know about predators. I have been a predator. I know how they think. I know exactly how to lead people. I know exactly how to march on people. I know human weaknesses. Why? Because I have been at the brunt end of all of them. I know them. And instead of laying down and dying and saying, "Well, this is my destiny, this is how God made me — I am just a leper, I am just a despotic, lying, deceiving leader — that the only reason that I feel good is if I have people around me that feed back into me so I can give them my rhetoric, which I myself don't even live" — I know human nature. I studied it all of my life. It was crucial for me to do that because I wanted to destroy everything that the God of my people made and abandoned. I thought the Unknown God had abandoned my mother, my people, Lemuria, had abandoned it for this despotic bunch of red-faced idiots here and on the moon and on Mars and God knows where else. It was one little boy who stood up and said no. An eagle rose up out of Lemuria and said no, not at forty-two or fifty but at fourteen. Fourteen years old, I was learning to wield a sword and watching and observing people because I wanted to exact a revenge. I was in love with revenge.

You see, that is why I understand about power and I understand the third seal and everything that falls under it, because the first seal is weak compared to the power of the third seal. It is, because all of you save for a few have fallen under the lie of love just to have sex with somebody. You have prostituted your own truth, your own value as a human being; you have prostituted the value of another human being in lying to them and telling them something sacred, that they would believe you and have trust. And even if they were idiots and innocent, no one should ever abuse innocence.

I know these things. I know what it is to be a God, and I know what it is to be a conqueror, and I know what it is to study people, men and women. I know you all. I know all the things you are hung-up on, I know all the things you think you are really terrific at, and I know all the lies that you tell. And I know all of the potential you haven't used, and I know more than anything the one thing that you need and want more desperately than anything in your life, and that is to know that elixir called love that gives us a vitality — that gives to us, doesn't take from us — that gives to us that immortal joy and peace of mind that allows us to have one voice in our head instead of fifty voices in our head. And love does that.

We have all the voices speaking in our head; we have no love in our life. We have only what we have done and what we are afraid to do. And we have put up all of these voices by doing this to everybody else. We are liars, we are cheaters, we are deceivers, and by the very act of deceiving somebody we create a voice in your head. The very act of contemplating a conquest, maneuvering and lying to them to get their body part, creates a voice because it is an experience that is now complete and now it has its say. So instead of wearing a crown of a thousand thorns we have but one voice, and one voice is that voice that is love that has brought us to this unifying moment in our life.

The Root of All Disease — The Lack of Love

Look at me. You say, "I don't need love." Right. Well, if you don't need love, why do you blame your parents, your friends, the places you are at, why are you on drugs, why do you shoot up, why do you take Ecstasy, why do you smoke marijuana, why do you overeat, why do you starve, why do you watch pornographic things? Why do you do these things? For attention, attention.

The person who believed you when you said you loved them, you say, "Well, it is their fault because they believed what I said." Well, you had the power in your hands and you didn't walk away from it. You indulged yourself. And what brought you to your knees and will be at your death is that you have abused the trust of another human being through not God — God is not blasphemous; God is incapable of being blasphemous — but love.

So we come then — If I haven't convinced you with my questions, my teachings and, of course, your subsequent answers to your partner, if love isn't important, then the quest for the Holy Grail may have been the bloodline of Jesus Christ, but even the Holy Grail had a great quest, and that was for the elixir of hummingbirds, the golden elixir of this magical feeling, love.

Rest assured this night if you have created your disease for attention, you did it because of the lack of love. But also understand this, that any moment that you retract your need for it outside of yourself, it can be accomplished within yourself.

So then along with my beginning teachings many years ago was not only that you are God but to love yourself, to love yourself as you have loved others. And of course here we get into the modus operandi of the nittus-grittus, because the way you have loved other people is that you have fantasized about them, you have spilt your seed, and you have lied to them, just like you are doing to yourself, and all along you are doing it to yourself. A being who learns to love themselves is an awkward journey, masters, because, remember, the voices are doing this,[1] and what you may love here is going to be objected here, what you love here is going to be objected there. That is the reason why there are so many voices, because some you love, some you hate, but the truth is they have all been loved into existence because you made them; you breathed into them the breath of life. You made that neuronet in your brain for love.

---

1 Arguing for attention and supremacy in our head.

194

So a man who tells a woman that he is in love with her, when he knows in the back of the brain all he wants to do, and yet he is compelled — And she wants to hear it, so after a while they have babies and they get married. And then once they live with each other, he realizes he is starting to make love at night to a woman that he fantasizes about. In other words, he is not making love to her anymore, and maybe she is not with him; maybe she is making breakfast. So then there comes, you know, the "Kuma Satra" or the *Kama Sutra*, or whatever it is called, the art of how to get gratification out of your partner. Now if you have to learn how to give gratification with feathers, bells, and whistles, then you ain't in love with this person. And I think nature took care of itself really well in just turning you on. I don't think we need any outside help, and if we do, we ain't turned on. How many of you understand that? Thank you. So be it.

So many of you are stuck with people that were just sexual. Many of you are stuck with people of pity. You just love this person but you kind of felt sorry for them, and because of your compassionate heart you are sucked into taking care of them — their whole disease, their whole trauma, their whole whatever — because that speaks to your compassionate heart. So will that person ever get well? No, no, no. If you are going to gain love because you are going to get sick, then chances are your attention you are going to misread as love, and so getting well would only mean the cost of that attention. Does that make sense to you?

Now are you in a relationship of compassion? And if you are, you are never going to get well. If you are in a relationship of understanding, you will never get well because the day you get well is when the understanding stops.

How many of you does that make sense to you? Remember, attitude is everything. That makes sense to you?

How many of you understand now why some people never get well in this school? Because they are addicted to the scenario of what their illness provides them, and in the end it all boils down — no matter all the adages — it boils down to love. They will get ill and die just because they will hunt at the table for scraps just to have that attention, that nourishment, that kindness, and that compassion.

Now you understand, but how many of you didn't understand all the sick people in my school and all the people that were obese and skinny, all the drug addicts? How many of you didn't understand people that would cling to absolutely adulterous people? You didn't understand that. You know why you didn't understand that? Because you thought you were the only person in this audience that had problems, so you never looked at anyone else; you only looked at yourself. That ain't love, baby; that is self-deceit. That ain't love, baby.

You didn't know that. All you wanted to do was ignore them because you couldn't help them and you knew you couldn't help them and, furthermore, you knew that you only cared about them when you were important in their life and they were important to you. But if you can't help them, you have a way of ignoring them, instead of just coming up to them and say, "You know what is wrong with you? You need some attention. Now what can we do to get you some attention?" I mean, you have been on this whole death fantasy, this whole sickness thing just to get some attention, and if the people in your life are not giving you anything, get rid of those — Get out of here and go to Barbados and get drunk for a month, spend all of your money, and dance on the tables.

If I were a really sick person, which I am not, I would understand this about myself: I would understand that I don't love myself and I am depending upon someone to mirror to me that love so I can feel it, and when the mirror doesn't catch the sunlight, I am busy searching the darkness to find the reflections of light. If I knew that about myself, that attitude is everything, then I would say to myself, "You know what? You are sick now because you were desperate to get somebody's attention. Your pride, my pride, was so great that I could never admit that, but subconsciously I felt it. I felt crippled by my own inadequacy of failure of my own philosophy, and to get attention." If I knew that about myself, people, and I knew that every beat of my heart was a countdown to my death and that I had so many beats left for my life to be this human being in this body — with this face, this body, these hands, these eyes, this heart, this mind — I would dump everybody and everything in my life and I would go and party and have the greatest time of my life until I never thought about them again. And when I had gotten sober from my great partying, after my great hangover, I would find I felt better than I ever felt in my life.

Oh, oh, oh, oh, this isn't spiritual? What do you think you know about spirituality? You treat spirituality as a separate subject from your life when in fact everything is Spirit, including your attitude, including your body, and including your environment. You don't love yourself when you have to go to the point to get sick for attention. You are powerless. And the only person you turn on — who do you turn on? — you turn on your body. Shame on you. Shame on you. No pretty face and no handsome body and no amount of money is worth dying for. No one is. That ain't a sign of self-love.

All disease is connected to inevitably the lack of love. And how we are taught that love is obtained is through the attentions of other people, and we are all whores — at least you are — and you are whoremongers just to get that bit of touch, that bit of elation, that bit of nakedness, that bit of intimacy. That ain't what it is about.

Power — The Ultimate Orgasm

Now if power — And as the old axiom says absolute power corrupts absolutely, then the greatest orgasm is not a sexual one; it is absolute power. That is the longest lasting orgasm there is, and those who have absolute power are in an absolute deluge of orgasmic activity for as long as their reign can hold. An orgasm, well, besides the foreplay and the petting, lasts about four thrusts. We hardly even know where it started and where it ended, but there it is; it is over with. Heavy, sticky breathing follows. "And I didn't even finish making breakfast in the morning."

But to lead people, be charismatic, to lead people, to instruct them, to teach them — the ultimate orgasm — is always the ultimate orgasm of any leader, and anything other than that, first or second seal, that is nothing. Power is absolute. That is the big orgasm. So how do you use that in your life? Well, in a myriad of ways. You abuse your power as a parent, you abuse your power as a lover, you abuse your power as a spiritual leader when through and through you are corrupt; you abuse yourself and abuse others. And the only reason you are a teacher is so that other people will pay attention to you, and if they pay attention to you, they surrender — think about it — they surrender their focus to you. That is powerful. That is why everybody wants to be famous because then everybody will focus on them, they will make all this money, they will be rich, and they will be loved by the world. And gurus do it because gurus are addicted to power. They don't know the first thing about God. Any guru that creates a devotee does not know about God. They only know about their need to be in power.

Well, if everyone told the truth, there would be no powermongers.

Now I want you to look — and in fact because I have brought it up you are going to have this manifestation in your life — that is to look at your partner and look at your attitude with your partner, and to look at your attitude to how many times you have not been present with that partner through the first-three-seals' experience or the first-two-seal experience. So be it.

Even the guru needs love. And even though power corrupts absolutely, in the end when you have everything you thought you needed, you always die lonely and empty, absolutely unfulfilled, never fulfilled, never fulfilled. The thirst is never quenched.

So what is love then? Well, it absolutely wasn't any of these things. It was as if — it was as if — something greater in our being allowed us to play this game that we took too shallow or too serious, and that all the while that which allowed us to play the game was the one who held the cards. Isn't that an apropos discussion?

You know, we talk about voices. I mean, all of you who were saying, "I love you and I really need you," how many of you were aware of something inside you that knew you weren't telling the truth? Raise your hands. Raise your hands. Thank you for your honesty. How refreshing. Isn't that an eerie feeling to know that your personality is saying something and then you are aware of something that knows that it ain't true? Isn't that an eerie feeling?

Student: Yes, and hopeful.

Ramtha: You know, she is right. So how many of you tonight are living the one voice instead of the many voices?

Now listen. Love is a many-splendored thing. It is like a diamond with many facets to it. But in order to love a diamond we cannot love the facets but the heart of the stone that gave its strength to allow this to be cut off from it, shaved, an experience, and allowed it to reflect light. The beauty of a diamond is its flawless center.

You Have Been Loved into Life

I had a very passionate sermon when I first appeared here and could barely speak this language. I had a very passionate sermon. It is still passionate today. And the sermon was that you are loved and that you are Gods and that you have been loved into life, a privilege in which you are squandering because of your addiction to your body, your addiction to your emotions, and your addictions to false neuronets in the brain, demons in the brain, that what you did before seems to now predetermine the future. If that is true, none of you have a future. It is only going to be more of the same.

Now how do we find love? In the first three seals our anatomy of mind and consciousness is this: We have a great field of consciousness that works in the brain to the dreams, and then we also have an anatomy of consciousness and mind in the brain that works to failure, that works to doubt, that wants to remember and never go forward. This part of the brain that does this is the one that is directly controlling the emotional body.

Now love then in our awkward stages would not be the love of our youth and in many cases would not be the love of our older years. But in our older years there is an ingratiating quality with older people, myself being one of them, and that is that when the hormones stop flowing to the first three seals, there is a relaxation in the mind that starts to occur. If the hormones are no longer turning on the first seal or turning on disease in the second seal or even wanting to have their voice heard on the third seal, if these hormones through age or cyclical changes of life are turned off, what does that do to this? And if old age brings us to a point of complacency, seemingly to our youth, if old age brings us to a point of absolute wisdom, if old age brings us to a point that we are no longer jealous of another person — we are no longer competitive to another person, if we are no longer struggling to be better than another person — if old age makes us grandmas and grandpas that give us warm bosoms and comfy tummies and strong arms and snowy white hair, then what it has done for us, it has finally eliminated our animalistic hormones and brought us to a state of grace, and a state of grace in which after living beyond the hormones in the body we have come to a point of clear-sightedness. And, yes, we have only come to the point that we ourselves were involved in.

So if we are only involved in a certain sector of our life, if we are only involved with religion, if we are only involved with trouble and difficulty or establishing a family or living to its creeds and its cultures, there comes a point — there comes a point — in golden years where we give it up. In our heart of hearts we give it up because we see that the driving force of religion itself was control over our hormones. We see indeed that illness was the driving force of our need to have our voice heard quietly but loudly. We see that in power and being stalwart and straight how we were unforgiving and ruthless and how we wanted everybody to believe in us and we were never wrong. Every old person realizes that, and that is all hormone-driven.

So they come to this — depending upon where they come from — this expediency in their elder years to where they see everything like as if they were a little child again but loaded with wisdom, and they are complacent only to the idealisms that they themselves were so responsible in setting forth in their own family. And very few of them come forward and say, "I was a fool; don't ever believe this way," but blessed are those who do.

And with that kind of age brings absolute nurturing, absolute wisdom, to look at everyone and never see them as a sexual opportunity — imagine that — to look at everyone and never imagine them as a sexual opportunity again, to look at people and to think, "My God, I would never get sick so as to burden my children, but I sure did this when I was a young person to get the attention of other people, and I don't want to do that now to my children." Every old person does not want to burden their children. You know why? Because they did this when they were young. They got the wisdom to understand that. That is beautiful. Self-pride, self-wisdom is wonderful.

And power, they are out of that game. They are out of that game; it doesn't mean anything to them anymore. Peace: To wake up every morning is remarkable, to have slept a whole night without pain or wakefulness or uncomfortableness, to wake up every morning and to shuffle around just so they can see the sun or the rain, that is the most important thing. And they think to themselves, "Damn, why didn't I do this when I was young? That is what they think. "Why didn't I do this when I was young? Why didn't I?" And they shuffle around. These are people who can absolutely live in the moment. That is why grandchildren love their grandparents. They love their grandparents because their grandparents are in the moment. They are not young anymore; they are not sexual anymore. They are not suffering; they don't want to suffer. They want to get up every morning, they want to make their own food, and they want to sleep all night long. These people may have suffered once, but they don't want to do it now. It is coming.

And bossy? No, they understand that their voice is not heeded anymore and so their need for power turns into love, or it can turn into powerful resentment, but love then starts at the third seal. But that which allowed you to play this loved you, but when you suspected that you weren't sincere, it is because something that was allowing it to happen knew you had made this choice. That is why you have always been uneasy with yourself. That is why living in your skin and in your brain has been uneasy, because when you think certain things, you always are aware that someone is listening. You are aware of that, and somehow you know that you have not made the greatest choice. You know that instinctively. That is correct; you haven't.

Now I was an old man before I ascended. Ramaya, who once had raven-black hair, had absolute snow-white, silver hair that drug the floor. My oldest daughter was an old woman. Imagine me: old man, old man, having a hard time breathing, sometimes a hard time talking — just because of my enlightening wound — snow-white hair, snow-white. In my later years my raven-dark hair turned snow-white. I looked just like my daughter, a couple of old cronies. That is good. When you see me with my black hair, you are going to see me as the warrior. But when you see me with a radiant light around my head, you are looking at my hair. It is pretty snowy. Did I go and dye it? No, I never did that. I was an old man when I finally got it together, too old to fight any more battles because the Spirit of doing that had left me. There was no passion in it, and I finally started to understand in my recovery what it was to conquer myself.

I know you haven't met this yet, but you will, because if you do not ascend you are going to die, and that means that before your death you are going to suffer and you are going to be incapacitated, and all of the silly things in your life will flow like tears from your eyes. And the hunt for sincerity will be white-hot in your mind and in your heart, white-hot. I know your hour is coming, and I want you to know that. It is. Surely as you sit here tonight, surely in moments away, your life is ending here, and what shall it be?

To fall in love with a person, another human being, has got to be the direct result of first falling in love with you, and that means that if you are this consciousness, these voices here, you already know now that this, your God, allowed this to happen. And how can we say that God tolerated this or let this happen or you needed to think this way? God is not a brainwasher, you know, regardless of what the Republicans say. God is not a brainwasher. No, it is love, love. Love allowed this explorative consciousness to happen. But unfortunately a few emotional events and it gets cast into stone, and then everybody stops growing and then we have reincarnation because we wear out the bodies, but the lessons are unfulfilled. We wear out bodies emotionally, not through the lack of exercise but through the lack of mental exercise. We wear out the body: It dies, we are still stuck with the same program, we have to have a new body, we go through it lickety-split, it dies, we are still stuck with it. This is just a little body. You are just another body. No matter what your altered ego says, you are temporal. And if you think you are not, I have a bridge I want to sell you.

No, it is the mind that wears out the bodies. I don't care how much you exercise, you ignorant fool; that is not the answer. Don't get me started. No. Look at me. You all want love, the great fountain, the great elixir. It is true, to have that magic moment we would lay down our lives for lifetimes to relive it but for an hour. It is that great of a high, and it is that quintessential of an orgasm. To love ourself is the beginning of the quest.

Rather, Do to You What You Do to Those You Love

Do you love yourself enough to do to yourself what you have done to estranged lovers who promised you all these things — you gave your body, your virginity, your bank account, you gave everything to? Would you be willing to do that to you? What is the criteria of your love: You like men, you like women, you don't like either? What is it? What distinguishes you from the normal? Maybe you are abnormal. Maybe — maybe — it is how you have twisted your mind.

Look at me. Would you as a parent expect your child from your womb, from your seed — look at me — would you have them do to themselves what you have been doing to yourself? It is a fair question because in the next life that is going to be the great experience. Would you? Come on. Come on. Would you? Would you? Why? Come on. Would you expect your child to get emotionally ill just to get back at you, your partner, or someone else? Would you? Would you encourage that? Would you encourage your child to believe a line of sexual fantasy about themselves? Would you encourage them to believe that? Would you? Would you encourage your child to go out and, like a predator, to seek sexual love and sexual favors? Would you? Would you? Would you like this done to your daughter what you have done to other women?

Would you like this done to your sons what other women have done to your sons? Would you? I am asking you. So why is it all right for you and not all right for them? Because you love them. Partners can come and go, but when you have passed your seed to the next generation, that is a love that cannot be broken by any sexual partner, the man for his children, the woman for her children; is absolute. Why would you do that to you and not allow that to your children? Because you love your children. Your children are an extension of your good. That is how you see them. They are an extension of your good. You take on all the bad but they are the good, and so you are going to preserve for them good and protect them against people like you. Yes, people like you. You love them.

All right. Children are not broken up into little boys or little girls; they are called children. That is a blanket consciousness for a treasure, that which is protected and fought for. And unless you have had children you will never understand what we are talking about here. But if you are a parent, you get an idea of the love I am talking about. Now when do you begin to feel that about yourself? When do you allow your Observer to tackle your voices and be as protective with you as you are with your children? When is the day that you no longer have to give in to your sexual voices, your diseased voices, your power voices — because they are just in your head — the same way that you would be a good steward to your children? Now this is a runner I am going to send you most powerfully in my audience. So be it.

To love you, to love you; why don't you love you? I will tell you why, because you have got a voice in your head that said "lay down, I think I love you." You have got another voice in your head that says, "I believe you are telling me the truth." You have got another voice in your head that says, "Everything is okay; this is just an experience." No responsibility; you have got that voice in your head. Then you have another voice in your head that feels bad because nobody took care of you. And you know who didn't take care of you? You.

But that cry of freedom that "everything is all right; everything is all right," well, hypocrisy and lies are not all right. So what hypocritical voice you have got going on in your head, people, that is telling you, "It is cool; this is a learning" — yeah, right — how many times do you have to do the learning, or is that simply a cover story for an addiction? And the greatest failing of all is that you have convinced yourself with these voices that this is the standard quote. And you know what breaks your heart is that there is no voice in your head that stands up to the lot of them. And what hurts — hurts — is that no one in your head was ever on your side, just like our first "lay down, I think I love you" ends up that there is nothing that we hear in our head that has compassion and love for us. That breaks my heart, and it should break yours too. It should break yours too.

Yes, you have got this voice, speaks this, speaks that, says this, "This is wrong; this is right." Oh, you love me until I talk about your truth, and then you don't love me. You go away, and that is cool; you are away from me. You know what? You ain't got no voice in your head to love you into life. You have got only first-seal neuronet, first-seal emotion. You have got second-seal neuronet: body, pain, suffering, accidents, disease, anything to gratify what is not happening within you. You are making it at the cost of your life. Third seal, everyone — everyone — is a potential to me: power, slavery, victimization, tyranny, religion, politics, royalists, communists, socialists, fascists, isms, isms, isms.

Listen to me. Our greatest hurt is that we didn't have a

voice loud enough that spoke up against all of our neuronets. That breaks our heart, so we cultivated a voice that always shouted down our greatness and spoke for our humanity. That is when we have lost God, because the voice of God is the Observer, a really soft little voice. It is kind. It is a whisper. It is like butterflies in your soul and in your mind. That is how quiet it is. And what we find about our ill-spent youth and into our adulthood, which we are sorely unprepared to have, why we don't like ourselves is because we have no one in our mind that sits up and speaks for us — we have no voice that says to us, "I love you, you are precious to me, don't do this, we will do better without it, you are a good girl, you are a good guy, you are a good boy, you have a good life, don't do this" — that speaks as old and as wise as the young, virulent voices that trash everything for gratification.

And, masters, this is what hurts the most: Every day of your life you are getting older. So, young people, you don't think you are getting older? What a fool you are. You are getting older. And as you get older, our madness starts to set in because we don't hear the voice of God. We have no willful voice — listen to me — that is so righteous and so kind and so moral and so loving that it can help this tattered brain to make its way through the labyrinth of its own deeds. And that is absolute hopelessness.

Hey, you think God is in a church? Do you think God is in a tabernacle? You think God is in a pile of ruins? You think God is in the cross? God is in you. The holiest relic there ever was was a little mirror — it is not the cross; it is a mirror — just for you to look at yourself in, to be reminded that the voice is coming from within your face and is talking to you. That is love.

And the disappointing thing is and why you are here

is because that voice ain't been so strong in your life. And the voice that is the great parent, the great father, the great mother — the voice of wisdom in your head that allows you to be foolish but says, "Now pay attention, don't go out here tonight, this is not a good thing, stay home" or "Go there, don't stay home, go there, go to wherever, go have yourself a few drinks, I will talk to you if you are getting into trouble; thank you very much, thank you very much, thank you very much" — that is the voice of God.

The sadness is that many of you are so doubting and so strict and so intellectual that you don't even hear it, and yet it is so small it allowed your voice to get that large, allowed your attitudes to get that large. The love of God, this, is the greatest love there is, and parenting that produces children is a reflection of the God that created us. It is called reflective love.

So what is then love in the fourth seal? Love in the fourth seal, how can I explain that to you without every adjective not having an anti-preposition to it? How can I explain that to you? How can I explain the fifth plane to you? How can I explain the sixth plane to you? More importantly, if you haven't heard the voice, how can I explain the seventh plane?

So what is it when we really fall in love? How should we approach this, and should we? Yes, you should, because the first step of the way is to clean yourself up, to love yourself as much as you would love a child in your family, and to do to you what you would do to a child, do to you. Throw away people, places, things, times, and events, and trash, get rid of them, get rid of it, everything. If your parents say you cannot see those children anymore, and they are wise, what are you going to do when the voice in your head says don't go there anymore? Are you going to say it is archaic, it is out of fashion, it is not cool? When we learn to listen to the voice, we will understand that godly love is liken unto parental love, and we don't go there and we follow that voice. I don't care how unconventional, how ignorant, how buffoonish it sounds, we don't go there. That is how we empower the one voice.

The Magic of Finding Our Perfect Mirror

How do we fall in love? Falling in love is first to have worked upon ourselves, honed in ourselves. We cannot fall in love if we are begging illness, if we are begging death, if we are begging sickness, if we are begging poverty, if we are begging victimization. We don't fall in love; we only get relief, but that is not love. We have to work on ourself and we have to love what we are, like we would love us as children. We cannot look at our face in the mirror and say it is too fat or it is too old or it is ugly, my nose is too big or my eyes are too far apart or my eyes are black and blue is pretty, or blue is ugly and black is beautiful. We can't take ourselves apart like that. We have to love us like we would love a child of ours that suckles at our breast or is protected in our great arms.

We have to learn that propaganda to the world is that the most beautiful people are already found — they are already found — and they just simply live up to an ideal of commercialism. As soon as they get one wrinkle in their face, they are out of here and they are no longer beautiful. That is not your story. You wouldn't cast away your child because your child was not socially beautiful; at least my confidence in you is that you wouldn't do that and that your child is yours. Love is its own beauty. Body parts don't make beauty. Soul and Spirit make beauty. To have a child that comes from your loins, your semen, your eggs, a living, breathing incarnating Spirit that came from you, it is a miracle. Who would not love this child because they were not photogenic or they had big thighs or an oblong face or they didn't have hair or they had too much? If you did, shame on you. Accursed is you, and to these things you will be in your next lifetime. That is a fact. You know why? Because what we resent and hold secret in this life builds the temple and the model of your next incarnation. I promise you, that is how it works.

What do we do when we fall in love? When we have worked on ourself, when we have rooted out our secrets, found the source of our anger, rooted out our self-guilt, told the truth, because you can't love someone when you are battling your own guilt. To make them be your redeemer is idiocy. You have to do it yourself. You have to clean the vessel. That means that you have put all your attention to you, and you take your life apart and you put it back together again. Change the way you live, please. Please. Love is not what goes in your mouth. It isn't about how much food you can consume. It isn't about how much sex you have. It isn't about how cool you look. It isn't about how much money you have. It is all waste. It all turns to crap.

Now I will tell you the greatest love affair there ever was is God loving you into life and having the patience to allow you to be alive, you who have squandered it through pizza and beer, squandered it through all of your addictions. Your heart is still beating — amazing, amazing. Amazing your heart is still beating.

So when we have cured ourself, we know the only reason we are sick is because of our attitude, and it stinks, and we change it. We start being active in our life. We start forgiving ourselves by telling the truth, that we can forgive. We do. We hold no secrets. We have no monkeys on our back. And, oh, yes, the cost of telling the truth is a good relationship, money in the bank, a new truck, a new car, a garden. Telling the truth has consequences but they ain't nothing compared to what, in the quantum world, that which we hide and suppress we are doomed to become, and the next incarnation will be built exactly on that.

Did you know that all of the years that you have lived in this body that you have had great lives and you have had lousy lives, lousy, bloodsucking, leeching lives? So why is it if you were really great in one life you were such a louse in the next? Because being great in the one life was at the cost of suppressing a lot of things, just like a clever politician does. And in the next life you are that which is suppressed, and it doesn't look so good. Do you understand?

Look at me. Mind does not die. Mind does not die. Flesh and blood will pass away, but the kingdom of heaven shall never pass away. Mind never passes away. All reincarnation is is the need to keep picking up lives that we can burn out, hoping to get to a conclusion of wisdom. Yes, you didn't hear that. Well, that is about right. And you probably won't ever realize this till some years after I am gone, and you will go, "My God, why didn't I realize that then?" Well, because you didn't want to realize that you are just an ongoing drama machine and you change more costumes than are in a Shakespearean play. You burn out bodies, but the mind goes on. And all we are looking for is that perfect marriage.

So to love, the greatest example is that we are the product of a great parent, not our partner, not our mate. You are the product of a great parent who has allowed you to be here stuffy, limited, ignorant, buffoonish, and on a bandstand preaching about your physical immortality, and all the while the wisdom of the ages is listening to this speech because it has heard it before. It ain't going to happen.

So what happens when we fall in love? Well, it is a lot different than sexual magnetism and it is a lot different than feeling sorry for somebody and it is a lot different than being drawn to a charismatic person. Falling in love is not this at all. When you really fall in love — and that is only a saying — what it really means is that love starts at the fourth seal up. It isn't down here.[2] This is pure animal. I will tell you why.

When we find a person whose mind mirrors our own — mirrors: their thoughts are our thoughts, our thoughts are theirs, not because they want to be, because they naturally are — when you find a person who thinks as highly of you as you do of yourself and vice versa, the magnetic power of mind to mind is billions of years transcendent of sexual attraction. No one here has found mind to mind, but many are close. When we find our greatest mystery, our greatest hope — which is ourself — finally reflected in another one, we are confused; is it the other or is it myself? It is the same. That is when we love. Let me tell you something: If we can find someone that stares back at us as much as we stare in a mirror, we will know love.

Now is it true opposites attract? Well, absolutely. For mating purposes that is a necessity. People are attracted because they are different in the first seal. People are attracted in the second seal because there is a need and a demand. In the third seal people are attracted because someone controls your life so you don't have to. But in the mind we are attracted because we have found the perfect mirror of our own mind. We are turned on with profound respect, admiration — listen to me —

2 The first three seals of sexuality, suffering, and manipulation.

respect, admiration, all divinity. This is how we hold the great mind. We don't want to even tarnish this with having sex; we have to get down there in the basement to do it. What turns us on is something about this other person that allows us, as if somebody cleaned the mirror and finally we are seeing ourself, and they vice versa. That is where true love is.

When you fall in love, it will not be over sexual attraction. It won't have anything to do with sex, as much as you argue for that; it won't. It will have to do with absolute mind, absolute power, and absolute reflection. And if you don't have that in your life, poor you, you have just got body parts. When you have that, and to approach it just to be with it, to speak with it, to look at it, to be in awe with it is how you feel about your own sacred self. You would never denigrate your own sacred self because through self-denigration is why you don't hear the voice. It breaks your heart that nothing in your head tells you to stand up and fight. Nothing in your head says you are better than this. There is no voice in your head that says to you you are worth living. There is no voice in your head that says that you are greater than this act. There is no voice in your head that says no. When we fall in love, we are getting to experience an anatomy of love that is the awakening of that little voice in another person. And it doesn't start from between our legs; it starts up here. And every seal coming from here down is explored, not this long trench from here up.

Everyone thinks you have got to go to bed and show them you are a great lover so that they will accept you. I will tell you that I find that as primitive as animals that have not understood the noble art of mating. It is far greater to get to know a person, to know their mind, to communicate with them, and once we know that mind, that will tell us if we go any further. To do anything else is simply to blow our semen away, is simply to give our body to another person to ravish. And I don't think that is what falling in love is about.

So will you have that? It is my most utmost desire that you have that. It is my utmost desire for you to find a woman in your life whose mind is like a steel trap, whose wonder is more beautiful in the far reaches and far corners and valleys of thought and concept, mixed in with dreams and will, or with a man — a man, no matter what he looks like — to find that man who is handsome and is noble and, as regal-looking as he is, does not fall to his lowest denominator and act like lions in heat, act like hyenas in heat, a pack of dogs doing it in the junkyard. This is a man that, unlike any other man, could easily be these things but is not, but understands them not with a force of control but simply that it is not important, but still that this man who has dreams, whose Spirit speaks through his mouth, whose passion vibrates the beating of his heart, whose concept of humanity, his place with humanity, his understanding, his love of God, his nobility of — A man who loves truth more than deception is rare. A man who loves greater than his loins is rare. When we find such a man, a noble man — I mean, they have been all through history. It doesn't mean they are gay. Just because they don't have sex doesn't mean they are gay, just noble men. And to know their mind, I mean, you have to get your vibration up there to get into that mind. This is a man that is not a victim, a warrior, but a peacemaker at the same time. It is a man who tills his own field, brings in his own food, creates his own kingdom, and is responsible for joy in that kingdom and protecting that kingdom. That is a great man. And in that is a quality for all people. They are very rare to find. When you find that man and you recognize him, then maybe you are the lady who long has wanted to find such a man, and maybe you are the lady the man has longed to find, a truly polarized situation that really is a oneness in mind.

You have a lot of work to do. You have to stop being sick. You have to stop fantasizing that somebody is going to pay because you are hurting. You are too costly. Get over it. Stop breeding like dogs and start asking yourself, "Is the sexual revolution a good thing for me? In an environment of AIDS, in an environment of gonorrhea, in an environment of herpes is this a good thing for me to be this free and open like everyone wants me to? Maybe I am being told that for a reason. Maybe if I am 'duh' enough I am going to be one of the casualties, and so I won't be able to live my days out into the new years of prosperity." Maybe that is what is going on. Could be.

Stop it. You could say, "Well, I can't help it. It comes over me." Oh, don't give me that. You can help everything that goes on in your body. With the moment becoming the Observer, you stop everything. Don't tell me that. Don't. Love yourself. Don't lay with trash. Don't say "I love you" and break a person's trust. Never do that. Never. And don't lay with people and thinking about other people. Don't do that. That is not having control in your reality. That is compromise. That is an injustice to yourself. And don't do things to be famous. Famous people are never real. They aren't real. They are — they are — like mirages. They look a certain way until you get closer and closer and the mirage disappears, but when you move away, it replaces itself. Don't want to be anything other than you.

Listen to me. Come to terms with your past religion. Come to terms with your creed. Come to terms with your bloodlines. Come to terms with your ethnic background. Come to terms with your sexuality. And the voices are going to rage now for a fortnight in your head, and what are you to do, to get manic and depressive and order ten more pizzas, two or three gallons of ice cream? Why don't we just bring the cow in and you live with the cow in your house? It would save a lot more energy if you did it that way. Don't do that. They are going to rage. You know why? Listen to me. I can tell you what broke my heart is that I hated without conscience — broke my heart — I hated without conscience, a fourteen-year-old absolute warrior not afraid of anything, no conscience. I hated without conscience. You know what that was? I had no voice in my head. I had nothing that reined me in. I had nothing to rely upon except an old teacher. Another human being gave me conscience. The greatest disappointment was that I didn't already have that in my head. In the end we find that the greatest heartaches are not what other people did but what we failed to do for ourselves. I can tell you from experience.

I didn't understand what that lady told me that gave me that sword and said conquer myself. Conquer myself? Tell a fourteen-year-old to conquer themselves, especially with my rage and my presence of being, everyone else is going to get conquered — not me, them — me against them.

My greatest pain was in my enlightenment to realize I was so dead and had no voice that spoke to my compassion and that spoke to my love and that spoke to my nobility, that I gained these traits through bloody murder without remorse — the danger that is happening in your children today — without remorse. The greatest pain in my life was that I didn't have the Bel Shanai, who gave me the sword, talking to me in my head. And it will be your greatest regret too. Conscience has always been referred to as God's angel. I had no angel, and I spent the rest of my life trying to find it and did.

When we find out our greatest treasure — to be in love with another person, to be in love with ourself — when we are in love with that person, it is because we are in love with ourself. We expect nothing from them that we wouldn't expect of ourselves. We ask not of them anything that we wouldn't ask of ourselves. We expect from them what we expect from ourselves. How do I know this? How can you be in love with these voices as an orchestra in your head? Who is going to love and for how long? One voice, that is the mastery. That is the Great Work, one voice, one voice. In one voice we will find love, we will find the genuine article. One voice. If we say that we are in love but we have all of these voices in our head, then we are only in love with someone who has got just as many voices in their head. True love comes down to one. Mastery along the way is to master all of those till we get to only one, and this is what I was after all of my life.

CLOSING WORDS
Could This Be Truly a Spiritual Teaching?

Ramtha is irreverent. I am irreverent to everything you think is spiritual because everything is spiritual. There is no thing, not even a thought-form, that does not originate in superconsciousness. Everything is. So how can we isolate all of your life and make you a little nun or a little nunnette? And I was a pretty strict cat in my life. All right, I understand that kind of discipline.

I know that you think it is terrible because no spiritual teacher would teach this way, but actually I have to tell you that only spiritual teachers would teach this way, only them. I mean, not to address the human condition is really being out of reach and a little artificial. Actually a lot of artificiality goes on. That is called, you know, that is called the power lunch. But to watch people sit there in their spiritual robes and their anointed oils and their eyes rolled up and their hands full of peace, you know, and I know what went on in their brain. I mean, they are sitting there giving the posture of ideal spiritual journey. I know what kind of animal lives inside these people. You see, they don't want to show anybody that because then they will be just like everybody else, and the whole idea for this artificial, orgasmic experience going on is to be different than other people. So in spiritual life we have to be a cut above and we have to be a little mysterious and a little remote and so we need to change our garment, our language, our kohl, our underwear, our hair, certain sacred things we wear, and we never crap our breeches

— that is being a little cut above — and we sit there over our walnut, and we talk about God and this and that and this and that. When we are stripped down, our fear is to be common. But unless you can be common, you will never know God.

So I have — I have and will always have — a unique place in world history. I will be one of the first spiritual teachers that didn't rape and do mouth — or how do I want to say this? — first-seal mouth resuscitation on their devotees, to blow them up with my own importance. I will be one of the first great gurus that didn't expect you to give all your possessions to me. I will be one of the first great teachers that could love you as much when I started as when I end, to choose rock-and-roll over the *Rock Of Ages*. Oh, you ain't never going to meet another teacher like me, you ain't never, because, like they say, when they made me they threw the pattern away, or at least I took it with me and hold it in a secret place.

All life is spiritual. That is what you don't understand. Spiritual people strike this pose that they are extraordinary. They don't smoke, and they don't chew, and they don't go with boys that do. Please. They eat salt, they eat seed, they eat thoughts, and they eat minds, and do other deeds. I mean, that ain't what we are out here for.

I want so much to close the gap between God and life. And the certain things you can't do, you shouldn't be doing them; you should be doing greater things. You know, there are people in this world — including you — that, you know, you have this sort of ordinary, boring life, you know, and it is really boring because you know why? Because everyone you talk to understands what you are going through. That is how common and boring it is. Now that is pretty boring, you know. And after what you have heard in these audiences, in this ground and on this stage, you now know you are pretty common. We have exposed a lot of stuff up here, and with that this kind of goes flat; some things kind of go flat after that. But the truth of the matter is, people, is that what isn't spiritual? Many people have these very common lives and they create secrets sometimes so that they will be special, and that they do vulgar things for their "Ooh!" You know, please, I want to see you — hell, I want to see you make Toyotas in the field;[1] I don't want to see you fart. I don't want to see you do adultery for the zillionth time in your life. I want to see a Toyota manifest in that field. Now that would be terrific, I mean, truly orgasmic.

You don't understand that this enormous gap between God and your life has been a chasm. But the truth is why do you have this silly life? Because something adores you; this adores you. The little voice adores you, loves you, and depends upon you to fly past the moon at night and to do great things, have adventures. And this whole stage, this whole prop, this whole prop of the Earth is all set up for your drama. So what isn't spiritual? What isn't there without consciousness and energy? What isn't? Everything is here. The broken beer bottle on the side of the desert is consciousness and energy.

So what is the spiritual life, the life to where you work, drink a little on Wednesday night, play cards on Friday night, go out, go to the movies, go to the dance hall on Saturday night and really tie it on, and on Sunday repent? I mean, is that the way it is supposed to be? No, I don't think so.

You haven't done anything wrong. As bad as the things we have heard here today, they are really actually more common. Thank God I am saying that, because there are many people that told truth here tonight, that many people here would not have had the courage to stand up and say, but feel much more

---

1 That is, manifest a car out of thin air through the power of the mind.

comfortable because someone did. That is a good thing. That doesn't mean you are bad. What is difficult is when you take this gift, this great gift — this great gift — and you retard it back to some predictable program in your life. Then you say, "This is my life, and then I am going to come to school once a year, I am going to go to church every Sunday, I am going to support foreign children, I am going to support the building of the new church," because it feels good for you to give spiritually. You feel good. "I am going to do this because, you know what? It makes me feel good. Because of all the other things I have done, it feels good to sort of feed my soul now and to feed my mind, because I don't have too much of that in my life, if you know what I mean."

Before I am gone here I want every one of you to know there is not one thing in your life that isn't spiritual, not one thing. What is missing is special attention to the one who is given this privilege to live, and how it is lived, and to understand if we talk about the ultimate lover, the ultimate lover is keeping your heart beating tonight. I have gotten to live the twenty-first century, and what a ride it has been. My greatest teaching to you is, what I started out to the toast tonight, how much I love you.

When we are moving energy, like climbing a ladder, the first rung is closest to our stability. We don't risk a lot when we take the first step, because where we started is right there. But as we continue up, we get further away from right there and we get into a little bit more risky, risqué territory. But what is so wonderful about taking a chance is it does take us further away from right there and lets us start to have a different view of things.

I could never, ever have told you in my life that I loved you. I never said that to any person because I didn't feel it. I didn't love anybody. I loved the Unknown God because it is my ultimate challenge but, no, and then my heart got softened with my children; then I started to feel a little more parental. And as years waned on, you know, and great losses and great victories and barely making it and the earth falling behind our heels and, you know, where once there was a valley now there is a river, and now the river has turned into an ocean — powerful times. Man, I lived through it. I know what it is. I mean, the wisdom of a wise man is worth — is worth — that which in opposition is many lives of an ignorant man who has experienced none of it. I have experienced these things. I came from violent times. And, in a way, a long time ago so did you.

When I tell you I love you — and, as you can tell, I am not quite finished with my message because I am struggling here with how my mind has to move through the brain to figure the words — when I tell you I love you, that means that I moved out of my third seal, the most powerful warlike being, and slowly made my way through a lot of suffering, a lot of suffering and a lot of reflection. But one thing I had, will, a sword, a wonder — I wondered; I had wonder — is to come to this place, that when I got up into my head, how could I ever love singular Ramtha anymore and not love everyone else? To my wonder that is what I came to, and so will you one day. You are isolated, suffering selves thinking no one else understands you, but as the truth is brought out more and more, you see how common you really are. And once that commonality is seen, perhaps then you will reach for the stars.

I send you the runners from the Lord God of my being on the true nature of love. It is quoted that Christ said no greater love hath any man than one who should lay down his life for another. That is true. The greatest love — the greatest love — is to give up your life that another can live, because ultimately you will live again. Why do we call this love? No greater love hath a man than he should lay down his life that another should live; that is beautiful because that shows us the height of the dizzy, wonderful, freeing consciousness that love is, because it will always live. Lives are temporal, but love is eternal.

And so this whole Ramtha journey has been about doing exactly that, and that, my beloved, is true love. So I send you the runners and I send you the gift, and maybe laying down your life is as simple as changing the attitudes that run your life, and if you can do that, then you have found self-love.

You all want love, the great fountain, the great elixir. To love ourself is the beginning of the quest. Attitude is everything, and you can do this. So be it.

Always yours,

Ramtha

EPILOGUE
Introduction to Ramtha by JZ Knight

*"In other words, his whole point of focus is to come here
and to teach you to be extraordinary."*

You don't have to stand for me. My name is JZ Knight and I am the rightful owner of this body, and welcome to Ramtha's school, and sit down. Thank you.

So we will start out by saying that Ramtha and I are two different people, beings. We have a common reality point and that is usually my body. I am a lot different than he is. Though we sort of look the same, we really don't look the same.

What do I say? Let's see. All of my life, ever since I was a little person, I have heard voices in my head and I have seen wonderful things that to me in my life were normal. And I was fortunate enough to have a family or a mother who was a very psychic human being, who sort of never condemned what it was that I was seeing. And I had wonderful experiences all my life, but the most important experience was that I had this deep and profound love for God, and there was a part of me that understood what that was. Later in my life I went to church and I tried to understand God from the viewpoint of religious doctrine and had a lot of difficulty with that because it was sort of in conflict with what I felt and what I knew.

Ramtha has been a part of my life ever since I was born, but I didn't know who he was and I didn't know what he was, only that there was a wonderful force that walked with me, and when I was in trouble — and had a lot of pain in my life growing up — that I always had extraordinary experiences with this being who would talk to me. And I could hear him as clearly as I can hear you if we were to have a conversation. And he helped me to understand a lot of things in my life that were sort of beyond the normal scope of what someone would give someone as advice.

It wasn't until 1977 that he appeared to me in my kitchen on a Sunday afternoon as I was making pyramids with my husband at that time, because we were into dehydrating food and we were into hiking and backpacking and all that stuff. And so I put one of these ridiculous things on my head, and at the other end of my kitchen this wonderful apparition appeared that was seven feet tall and glittery and beautiful and stark. You just don't expect at 2:30 in the afternoon that this is going to appear in your kitchen. No one is ever prepared for that. And so Ramtha at that time really made his appearance known to me.

The first thing I said to him — and I don't know where this comes from — was that "You are so beautiful. Who are you?"

And he has a smile like the sun. He is extraordinarily handsome. And he said, "My name is Ramtha the Enlightened One, and I have come to help you over the ditch." Being the simple person that I am, my immediate reaction was to look at the floor because I thought maybe something had happened to the floor, or the bomb was being dropped; I didn't know.

And it was that day forward that he became a constant in my life. And during the year of 1977 a lot of interesting things happened, to say the least. My two younger children at that time got to meet Ramtha and got to experience some incredible phenomena, as well as my husband.

Later that year, after teaching me and having some difficulty telling me what he was and me understanding, one day he said to me, "I am going to send you a runner that will bring you a set of books, and you read them because then you will know what I am." And those books were called the *Life and Teaching of the Masters of the Far East* (DeVorss & Co. Publishers, 1964). And so I read them and I began to understand that Ramtha was one of those beings, in a way. And that sort of took me out of the are-you-the-devil-or-are-you-God sort of category that was plaguing me at the time.

And after I got to understand him, he spent long, long moments walking into my living room, all seven feet of this beautiful being making himself comfortable on my couch, sitting down and talking to me and teaching me. And what I didn't realize at that particular time was he already knew all the things I was going to ask and he already knew how to answer them. But I didn't know that he knew that.

So he patiently since 1977 has dealt with me in a manner by allowing me to question not his authenticity but things about myself as God, teaching me, catching me when I would get caught up in dogma or get caught up in limitation, catching me just in time and teaching me and walking me through that. And I always said, "You know, you are so patient. You know, I think it is wonderful that you are so patient." And he would just smile and say that he is 35,000 years old, what else can you do in that period of time? So it wasn't really until about ten years ago that I realized that he already knew what I was going to ask and that is why he was so patient. But as the grand teacher that he is, he allowed me the opportunity to address these issues in myself and then gave me the grace to speak to me in a way that was not presumptuous but in a way, as a true teacher would, that would allow me to come to realizations on my own.

Channeling Ramtha since late 1979 has been an experience, because how do you dress your body for — Ram is seven feet tall and he wears two robes that I have always seen him in.

Even though they are the same robe, they are really beautiful so you never get tired of seeing them. The inner robe is snow white and goes all the way down to where I presume his feet are, and then he has an overrobe that is beautiful purple. But you should understand that I have really looked at the material on these robes and it is not really material. It is sort of like light. And though the light has a transparency to them, there is an understanding that what he is wearing has a reality to it.

Ramtha's face is cinnamon-colored skin, and that is the best way I can describe it. It is not really brown and it is not really white and it is not really red; it is sort of a blending of that. And he has very deep black eyes that can look into you and you know you are being looked into. He has eyebrows that look like wings of a bird that come high on his brow. He has a very square jaw and a beautiful mouth, and when he smiles you know that you are in heaven. He has long, long hands, long fingers that he uses very eloquently to demonstrate his thought.

Well, imagine then how after he taught me to get out of my body by actually pulling me out and throwing me in the tunnel, and hitting the wall of light, bouncing back, and realizing my kids were home from school and I just got through doing breakfast dishes, that getting used to missing time on this plane was really difficult, and I didn't understand what I was doing and where I was going. So we had a lot of practice sessions.

You can imagine if he walked up to you and yanked you right out of your body and threw you up to the ceiling and said now what does that view look like, and then throwing you in a tunnel — and perhaps the best way to describe it is it is a black hole into the next level — and being flung through this tunnel and hitting this white wall and having amnesia. And you have to understand, I mean, he did this to me at ten o'clock in the morning and when I came back off of the white wall it was 4:30. So I had a real problem in trying to adjust with the time that was missing here. So we had a long time in teaching me how to do that, and it was fun and frolic and absolutely terrifying at moments.

But what he was getting me ready to do was to teach me something that I had already agreed to prior to this incarnation, and that my destiny in this life was not just to marry and to have children and to do well in life but to overcome the adversity to let what was previously planned happen, and that happening including an extraordinary consciousness, which he is.

Trying to dress my body for Ramtha was a joke. I didn't know what to do. The first time we had a channeling session I wore heels and a skirt and, you know, I thought I was going to church. So you can imagine, if you have got a little time to study him, how he would appear dressed up in a business suit with heels on, which he has never walked in in his life.

But I guess the point that I want to tell you is that it is really difficult to talk to people — and perhaps someday I will get to do that with you, and understanding that you have gotten to meet Ramtha and know his mind and know his love and know his power — and how to understand that I am not him, and though I am working diligently on it, that we are two separate beings and that when you talk to me in this body, you are talking to me and not him. And sometimes over the past decade or so, that has been a great challenge to me in the public media because people don't understand how it is possible that a human being can be endowed with a divine mind and yet be separate from it.

So I wanted you to know that although you see Ramtha out here in my body, it is my body, but he doesn't look anything like this. But his appearance in the body doesn't lessen the magnitude of who and what he is. And you should also know that when we do talk, when you start asking me about things that he said, I may not have a clue about what you are talking about because when I leave my body in a few minutes, I am gone to a whole other time and another place that I don't have cognizant memory of. And however long he spends with you today, to me that will maybe be about five minutes or three minutes, and when I come back to my body, this whole time of this whole day has passed and I wasn't a part of it. And I didn't hear what he said to you and I don't know what he did out here. When I come back, my body is exhausted and it is hard to get up the stairs sometimes to change to make myself more presentable for what the day is bringing me, or what is left of the day.

You should also understand as beginning students, one thing that became really obvious over the years, that he has shown me a lot of wonderful things that I suppose people who have never gotten to see them couldn't even dream of in their wildest dreams. And I have seen the twenty-third universe and I have met extraordinary beings and I have seen life come and go. I have watched generations be born and live and pass in a matter of moments. I have been exposed to historical events to help me to understand better what it was I needed to know. I have been allowed to walk beside my body in other lifetimes and watch how I was and who I was, and I have been allowed to see the other side of death. So these are cherished and privileged opportunities that somewhere in my life I earned the right to have them in my life. To speak of them to other people is, in a way, disenchanting because it is difficult to convey to people who have never been to those places what it is. And I try my best as a storyteller to tell them and still fall short of it.

But I know that the reason that he works with his students the way that he does is because also Ramtha never wants to overshadow any of you. In other words, his whole point of focus is to come here and to teach you to be extraordinary; he already is. And it is not about him producing phenomena. If he told you he was going to send you runners, you are going to get them big time. It is not about him doing tricks in front of you; that is not what he is. Those are tools of an avatar that is still a guru that needs to be worshiped, and that is not the case with him.

So what will happen is he will teach you and cultivate you and allow you to create the phenomenon, and you will be able to do that. And then one day when you are able to manifest on cue and you are able to leave your body and you are able to love, when it is to the human interest impossible to do that, one day he will walk right out here in your life because you are ready to share what he is. And what he is is simply what you are going to become. And until then he is diligent, patient, all-knowing, and all-understanding of everything that we need to know in order to learn to be that.

And the one thing I can say to you is that if you are interested in what you have heard in his presentation, and you are starting to love him even though you can't see him, that is a good sign because it means that what was important in you was your soul urging you to unfold in this lifetime. And it may be against your neuronet. Your personality can argue with you and debate with you, but you are going to learn that that sort of logic is really transparent when the soul urges you onto an experience.

And I can just say that if this is what you want to do, you are going to have to exercise patience and focus and you are going to have to do the work. And the work in the beginning is very hard. But if you have the tenacity to stay with it, then one day I can tell you that this teacher is going to turn you inside out. And one day you will be able to do all the remarkable things that in myth and legend that the masters that you have heard of have the capacity to do. You will be able to do them because that is the journey. And ultimately that ability is singularly the reality of a God awakening in human form.

Now that is my journey and it has been my journey all of my life. And if it wasn't important and if it wasn't what it was, I certainly wouldn't be living in oblivion most of the year for the sake of having a few people come and have a New Age experience. This is far greater than a New Age experience. And I should also say that it is far more important than the ability to meditate or the ability to do yoga. It is about changing consciousness all through our lives on every point and to be able to unhinge and unlimit our minds so that we can be all we can be.

You should also know that what I have learned is we can only demonstrate what we are capable of demonstrating. And if you would say, well, what is blocking me from doing that, the only block that we have is our lack to surrender, our ability to surrender, our ability to allow, and our ability to support ourself even in the face of our own neurological or neuronet doubt. If you can support yourself through doubt, then you will make the breakthrough because that is the only block that stands in your way. And one day you are going to do all these things and get to see all the things that I have seen and been allowed to see.

So I just wanted to come out here and show you that I exist and that I love what I do and that I hope that you are learning from this teacher and, more importantly, I hope you continue with it.

— *JZ Knight*

Ramtha's Selected Glossary of Terms and Disciplines

For more information on Ramtha's teachings, his disciplines and techniques for personal transformation and focus, please visit or write to Ramtha's School of Enlightenment, P.O. Box 1210, Yelm, WA 98597, U.S.A., www.ramtha.com. Ramtha's book, *A Beginner's Guide to Creating Reality,* Third Edition (JZK Publishing, 2004), contains Ramtha's introduction to his teachings, his disciplines, and his School of Enlightenment.

Analogical Archery®: Discipline created by Ramtha to provide students immediate feedback of their ability to manifest reality. Students are taught to broaden and refine the focused power of the mind while blindfolded.

Analogical Mind: Being analogical means living in the Now. It is the creative moment and is outside of time, the past, and the emotions.

Bands, the: The bands are the two sets of seven frequencies that surround the human body and hold it together. Each of the seven frequency layers of each band corresponds to the seven seals of seven levels of consciousness in the human body. The bands are the auric field that allow the processes of binary and analogical mind.

Binary Mind: This term means two minds. It is the mind produced by accessing the knowledge of the human personality and the physical body without accessing our deep subconscious mind. Binary mind relies solely on the knowledge, perception, and thought processes of the neocortex and the first three seals. The fourth, fifth, sixth, and seventh seals remain closed in this state of mind.

Blue Body®: The body that belongs to the fourth plane of existence, the bridge consciousness, and the ultraviolet frequency band. The Blue Body® is the lord over the lightbody and the physical plane. It is also a discipline taught by Ramtha in which the students lift their conscious awareness to the consciousness of the fourth plane. This discipline allows the Blue Body® to be accessed and the fourth seal to be opened for the purpose of healing or changing the physical body. This technique is taught exclusively at Ramtha's School of Enlightenment.

Body/mind consciousness: Body/mind consciousness is the consciousness that belongs to the physical plane and the human body.

Book of Life: Ramtha refers to the soul as the Book of Life, where the whole journey of involution and evolution of each individual is recorded in the form of wisdom.

Candle Focus: Discipline taught by Ramtha to still the sensory and analytical mind and reach the state of analogical mind.

Consciousness & Energy — C&E®: "The breath of power." Abbreviation of Consciousness & Energy®. This is the service mark of the fundamental discipline of manifestation and the raising of consciousness taught in Ramtha's School of Enlightenment. Through this discipline the students learn to create an analogical state of mind, open up their higher seals, and create reality from the Void. A Beginning C&E® Workshop is the name of the introductory workshop for beginning students in which they learn the fundamental concepts and disciplines of Ramtha's teachings. The teachings of the Beginning C&E® Workshop can be found in *Ramtha, A Beginner's Guide to Creating Reality,* Third Ed. (Yelm: JZK Publishing, a division of JZK, Inc., 2004.) This technique is taught exclusively at Ramtha's School of Enlightenment.

Create Your Day®: Discipline created by Ramtha for raising consciousness and energy and intentionally creating a plan of events and experiences for the day very early in the morning before the activities of the day begin. This technique is taught exclusively at Ramtha's School of Enlightenment.

Fieldwork®: This is one of the fundamental disciplines of Ramtha's School of Enlightenment. The students are taught to create a symbol of something they want to know and experience and draw it on a paper card. These cards are placed with the blank side facing out on the fence rails of a large field. The students blindfold themselves and focus on their symbol, allowing their body to walk freely to find their card through the application of the law of consciousness and energy and analogical mind. This technique is taught exclusively at Ramtha's School of Enlightenment.

Grid®, The: This is the service mark for a technique created by Ramtha for raising consciousness and energy and intentionally tapping into the field of Zero Point Energy and the fabric of reality through a mental visualization. This technique is exclusively taught at Ramtha's School of Enlightenment.

JZ Knight: JZ knight is the only channel through whom Ramtha has chosen to deliver his message. Ramtha refers to JZ as his beloved daughter. She was Ramaya, the eldest of the children given to Ramtha during his lifetime.

List, the: The List is the discipline taught by Ramtha where the student gets to write a list of items they desire to know and experience and then learn to focus on it in an analogical state of consciousness. The List is the map used to design, change, and reprogram the neuronet of the person. It is the tool that helps to bring meaningful and lasting changes in the person and their reality. This technique is taught exclusively at Ramtha's School of Enlightenment.

Mother/Father Principle: It is the Source of all life, the Father, the eternal Mother, the Void. God the creator is seen as Point Zero and primary consciousness, which came out of the Void. The Source is the Void itself.

Neighborhood Walk®: Discipline created by JZ Knight for raising consciousness and energy to intentionally modify our brain's neuronet and preestablished patterns of thinking that we no longer desire and to replace them with new ones of our own choice. This technique is taught exclusively at Ramtha's School of Enlightenment.

Sending-And-Receiving: Discipline created by Ramtha to develop the brain's innate ability for telepathy and remote-viewing, both with a specific target or a partner, anywhere, anything, or any time, past, present, or future.

Seven Levels of Consciousness and Energy: The seven levels of consciousness and energy is Ramtha's model of reality and it explains our origins and destiny. It is expressed graphically as a triad, with the seventh level at the top and Point Zero at the apex. Consciousness and energy are inextricably combined and the seven levels of consciousness correspond to the seven levels of the electromagnetic spectrum. They also represent levels of energy, frequency, density of mass, space, and time. The levels or planes of consciousness and its energy from the first to the seventh are: 1. Subconsciousness and Hertzian; 2. Social consciousness and infrared; 3. Awareness and visible light; 4. Bridge consciousness and ultraviolet blue; 5. Superconsciousness and x-ray; 6. Hyperconsciousness and gamma; and 7. Ultraconsciousness and Infinite Unknown.

Seven Seals of Consciousness and Energy: The seven seals are powerful energy centers that constitute seven levels of consciousness in the human body. The bands are the way in which the physical body is held together according to these seals. In every human being there is energy spiraling out of the first three seals or centers. The energy pulsating out of the first three seals manifests itself respectively as sexuality, pain, and/or power. When the upper four seals are unlocked, a higher level of awareness is activated.

Tank®, The: It is the name given to the labyrinth used as part of the disciplines of Ramtha's School of Enlightenment. The students are taught to find the entry to this labyrinth blindfolded and move through it focusing on the Void without touching the walls or using the eyes or the senses. The objective of this discipline is to find, blindfolded, the center of the labyrinth or a room designated and representative of the Void.

Torsion Process®: Ramtha's technique to use one's mind to create a torsion field whereby one can build a wormhole in time/space, alter reality, and create dimensional phenomena such as invisibility, levitation, bilocation, teleportation, and others.

Twilight®, Visualization Process: It is the process used to practice the discipline of the List or other visualization formats. The student learns to access the alpha state in the brain with focused intent in a state similar to deep sleep, yet retaining their conscious awareness.

Unknown God: The Unknown God was the single God of Ramtha's ancestors, the Lemurians. The Unknown God also represents the forgotten divinity and divine origin of the human person.

Void, the: The Source. The Void is defined as one vast nothing materially, yet all things potentially.

About Ramtha's School of Enlightenment

Ramtha's School of Enlightenment (RSE), created by Ramtha the Enlightened One, is an academy of the mind.

Using ancient wisdom and the latest discoveries in neuroscience and quantum physics, RSE offers retreats and workshops and teaches students of all ages and cultures how to access the extraordinary abilities of the brain to "Become a Remarkable Life®."

Ramtha is a legendary Master Teacher who mastered his own humanity centuries ago and returned in our modern times to tell his story and teach us what he learned. He explains that in his lifetime he addressed the questions about human existence and the meaning of life, and that through his own observation, reflection, and contemplation he became enlightened and conquered the physical world and death. His philosophy reflects the experience of his own life. Ramtha's teachings are not a religion. They offer a unique perspective from which to view the mystery of life.

Ramtha's teachings emphasize that each individual is responsible for their own reality, that your thoughts and attitudes affect and create your life, and that you can intentionally change your life by artfully changing your thought.

Ramtha communicates his wisdom by channeling through the body of JZ Knight. JZ Knight began publicly channeling Ramtha in 1979. RSE was established in 1988 in Yelm, Washington, and more than 100,000 people from around the world have attended Ramtha's events.

JZ Knight is the unique channel of Ramtha and author of the best-selling autobiography, *A State of Mind, My Story*. Historians and religious experts who have studied her life's work call JZ Knight the Great American Channel and recognize her as one of the most charismatic and compelling spiritual leaders of the modern age. JZ Knight is the only channel through whom Ramtha has chosen to deliver his message. She and Ramtha have inspired audiences worldwide for the last three decades, bridging ancient wisdom and the power of consciousness together with the latest discoveries in science.

The home campus sits on 80 acres of pastoral, lush grounds and towering evergreens in Yelm, Washington. Great cedar and fir trees grace the grounds, and a sense of timelessness prevails. Events are conducted in the Great Hall, which can accommodate up to 1,000 students. RSE facilitates live events in many languages at the Yelm campus, at venues around the world, and via Internet streaming. For more information, please visit www.ramtha.com.

"What is the job of the Master Teacher? To give extraordinary knowledge, enough to make the human mind query questions that are no longer mundane but venture into the outrageous and the unfathomable, because when asking such questions, we awaken the Spirit and we awaken the true spiritual nature of ourself."

"You can do anything. The key is focus."

"One day I will have turned out Christs from this school and the world will rejoice, for this is the mission."

— Ramtha

LIST OF SOURCES

The excerpts from the various events that were used in the chapters of this book were left in their original dialogue format as they took place when they were delivered by Ramtha.

Chapter 1: Everyone Wants It. Everyone Craves It. But What Is It? was taken from *Finding Peace in Love,* Tape 478 ed. Yelm: Ramtha Dialogues, October 30, 2000.

Chapter 2: How Do You Make Love to a Woman? was taken from *A Teaching Dedicated to the Feminine Gender and Understanding Molecules of Intent and Becoming a Christ,* Tape 374 ed. Yelm: Ramtha Dialogues, February 20-24, 1998.

Chapter 3: Intimate Secrets of a Master was taken from *Miracles Exist Outside Emotional Time,* Tape 422 ed. Yelm: Ramtha Dialogues, September 28, 1999.

Chapter 4: Don Juan and Saint-Germain at the Countess' House was taken from *Miracles Exist Outside Emotional Time,* Tape 422 ed., and *Love Is a Many-Splendored Thing: Mastery and the Relationship Factor, Part I,* Tape 382.5 ed. June 26, 1998.

Chapter 5: True Beauty and Originality was taken from *Love Is a Many-Splendored Thing: Mastery and the Relationship Factor, Part I,* Tape 382.5 ed., and *A Teaching Dedicated to the Feminine Gender and Understanding Molecules of Intent and Becoming a Christ,* Tape 374 ed.

Chapter 6: Impact on Reincarnation was taken from *Finding Peace in Love,* Tape 478 ed.

Closing Words: Could This Be Truly a Spiritual Teaching? was taken from *Finding Peace in Love,* Tape 478 ed., and *Love Is a Many-Splendored Thing: Mastery and the Relationship Factor, Part I,* Tape 382.5 ed.

Fig. A: The Seven Seals:
Seven Levels of Consciousness in the Human Body

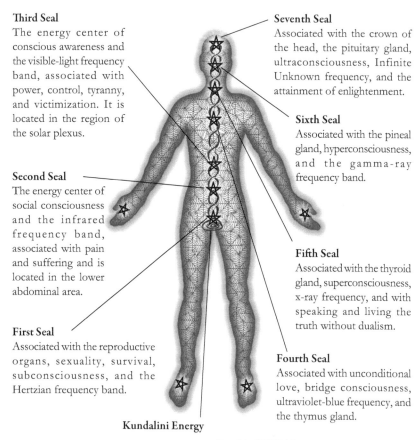

Third Seal
The energy center of conscious awareness and the visible-light frequency band, associated with power, control, tyranny, and victimization. It is located in the region of the solar plexus.

Second Seal
The energy center of social consciousness and the infrared frequency band, associated with pain and suffering and is located in the lower abdominal area.

First Seal
Associated with the reproductive organs, sexuality, survival, subconsciousness, and the Hertzian frequency band.

Seventh Seal
Associated with the crown of the head, the pituitary gland, ultraconsciousness, Infinite Unknown frequency, and the attainment of enlightenment.

Sixth Seal
Associated with the pineal gland, hyperconsciousness, and the gamma-ray frequency band.

Fifth Seal
Associated with the thyroid gland, superconsciousness, x-ray frequency, and with speaking and living the truth without dualism.

Fourth Seal
Associated with unconditional love, bridge consciousness, ultraviolet-blue frequency, and the thymus gland.

Kundalini Energy

Fig. B: Seven Levels of Consciousness and Energy

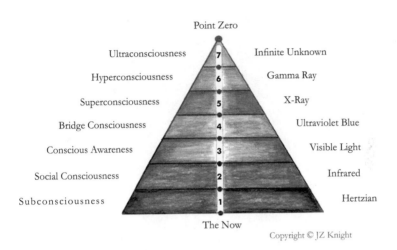

Copyright © JZ Knight

Fig. C: The Brain

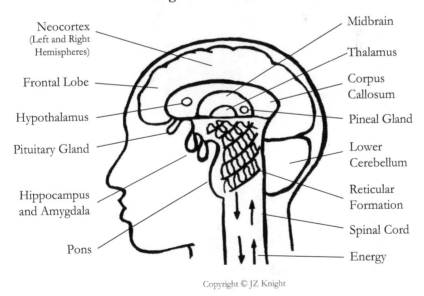

Copyright © JZ Knight

Fig. D: Binary Mind — Living the Image

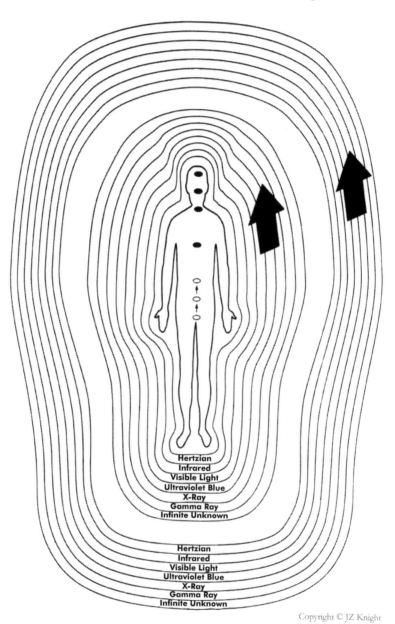

Hertzian
Infrared
Visible Light
Ultraviolet Blue
X-Ray
Gamma Ray
Infinite Unknown

Hertzian
Infrared
Visible Light
Ultraviolet Blue
X-Ray
Gamma Ray
Infinite Unknown

Fig. E: Analogical Mind — Living in the Now

Hertzian
Infrared
Visible Light
Ultraviolet Blue
X-Ray
Gamma Ray
Infinite Unknown

Infinite Unknown
Infinite Unknown
Infinite Unknown
Infinite Unknown
Infinite Unknown
Infinite Unknown
Infinite Unknown

Fig. F: The Observer Effect and the Nerve Cell

**The Observer is responsible
for collapsing the wave-function of probability
into particle reality**

Particle   Energy wave   The Observer

**The act of observation
makes the nerve cells fire and produces thought**

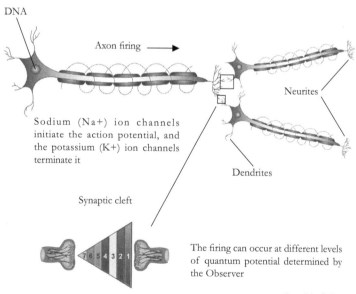

DNA

Axon firing ⟶

Sodium (Na+) ion channels
initiate the action potential, and
the potassium (K+) ion channels
terminate it

Synaptic cleft

Neurites

Dendrites

The firing can occur at different levels
of quantum potential determined by
the Observer

Fig. G: Cellular Biology and the Thought Connection

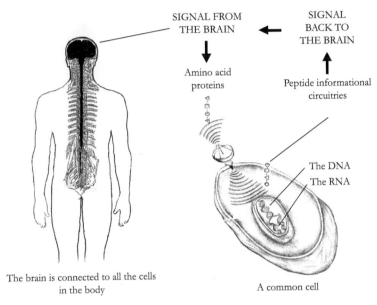

SIGNAL FROM
THE BRAIN

SIGNAL
BACK TO
THE BRAIN

Amino acid
proteins

Peptide informational
circuitries

The DNA
The RNA

The brain is connected to all the cells
in the body

A common cell

BIBLIOGRAPHY

Abbott, Edwin A. *The Annotated Flatland, A Romance of Many Dimensions*. Cambridge: Perseus Publishing, 2001.

Byron, George Gordon. *The Complete Poetical Works*. Edited by Jerome J. McGann, 6 Vols. New York: Oxford University Press, 1980.

Casanova, Giacomo, Chevalier de Seingalt. *History of My Life*. Translated by Willard R. Trask, 12 Vols. New York: Harcourt, Brace & World, Inc., 1966.

Hume, David. *An Enquiry Concerning Human Understanding*. Edited by Tom L. Beauchamp. New York: Oxford University Press, 1999.

Hume, David. *Essays Moral, Political, and Literary*. Edited by Eugene F. Miller, Revised Ed. Indianapolis, Indiana: Liberty Fund, Inc., 1987.

Krippner, Stanley, Wickramasekera, Ian, et al. *The Ramtha Phenomenon: Psychological, Phenomenological, and Geomagnetic Data*. In *The Journal of the American Society for Psychical Research*, Vol. 92, No. 1, January 1998.

Kuanghu Comber, Elizabeth Chow. *A Many-Splendored Thing, an Autobiography by Han Suyin*. Boston: Little, Brown and Company, 1952.

Molière. *Don Juan and Other Plays*. Translated by George Graveley and Ian Maclean. New York: Oxford University Press, 1998.

Molina, Tirso de, et al. *The Theatre of Don Juan. A Collection of*

Plays and Views, 1630-1963. Edited by Oscar Mandel. Lincoln, Nebraska: University of Nebraska Press, 1986.

Mozart, W. A. *Don Giovanni*. The Dover Opera Libretto Series Ed. New York: Dover Publications, 1976.

New American Bible.

Pert, Candace B. *Molecules of Emotion*. New York: Simon & Schuster Inc., 1997.

Ramtha, A Beginner's Guide to Creating Reality. Revised and Expanded Ed. Yelm: JZK Publishing, a division of JZK, Inc., 2000.

Ramtha, A Master's Reflection on the History of Humanity. Part I, *Human Civilization, Origins and Evolution*. Yelm: JZK Publishing, a division of JZK, Inc., 2001.

Ramtha, A Teaching Dedicated to the Feminine Gender and Understanding Molecules of Intent and Becoming a Christ. Tape 374 Audio Ed. Yelm: Ramtha Dialogues, 1998.

Ramtha, Finding Peace in Love. Tape 478 Audio Ed. Yelm: Ramtha Dialogues, 2000.

Ramtha, Love Is a Many-Splendored Thing: Mastery and the Relationship Factor. Part I, Tape 382.5 Audio Ed. Yelm: Ramtha Dialogues, 1998.

Ramtha, Miracles Exist Outside Emotional Time. Tape 422 Audio Ed. Yelm: Ramtha Dialogues, 1999.

Ramtha, The Emotional Body. Tape 9428.1 Audio Ed. Yelm: Ramtha Dialogues, 1994.

Ramtha, The Mystery of Birth and Death, Redefining the Self. Yelm: JZK Publishing, a division of JZK, Inc., 2000.

Ramtha, The White Book. Revised and Expanded Ed. Yelm: JZK Publishing, a division of JZK, Inc., 1999, 2001.

Ross, Colin A. *Dissociative Identity Disorder: Diagnosis, Clinical Features, and Treatment of Multiple Personality.* 2nd. Ed. New York: John Wiley & Sons, 1996.

Shaw, George Bernard. *Man and Superman: A Comedy and a Philosophy.* Edited by Dan H. Laurence. New York: Penguin Classics, 2001.

Spalding, Baird T. *Life and Teaching of the Masters of the Far East.* California: DeVorss & Co. Publishers, 1964.

Suetonius, *The Lives of the Caesars.* Translated by J.C. Rolfe, 2 Vols., Loeb Classical Library Ed. Cambridge: Harvard University Press, 1914.

Thompson, Francis. *The Poems of Francis Thompson: The First Complete Edition from Original Manuscripts and Published Sources.* Edited by Bridget Boardman. New York: Continuum International Publishing Group, 2001.

INDEX

A

abstinence 68, 122, 169, 185, 215

adultery 16, 29, 76, 139, 168, 223

aging 29, 59, 69, 102, 116, 157

alchemy 79-80, 111

altered ego 204

altered states of awareness 76, 91,
    118, 139, 177-179

amnesia 77, 96-102, 104, 106, 135

Ancient School of Wisdom 147,
    150-151

angel 217

animal instinct 16, 26, 35, 37-39,
    162-163, 170, 174, 184, 188,
    201, 213-214

ascension 90, 203-204

Atlatia 119

aura 115

awareness 16, 24, 31, 53, 57-58,
    69, 75, 91, 107, 137, 147, 152,
    168, 199, 201, 203, 225

B

barrenness 38, 137

beauty 18, 45-46, 50, 54-55, 57, 59,
63-65, 67-68, 70, 75-77, 114,
131, 137, 139, 146-147, 158,
165-166, 171, 185, 200, 210,
215

Bel Shanai 217

belief 14, 25

birth control 52

brain 71, 87, 93-94, 97-100, 102-
    105, 124, 140, 151, 160, 169,
    183, 194-195, 200, 203, 208,
    221, 225

frontal lobe 92, 140, 159

lower cerebellum 93-94

neocortex 149

breath of life 26, 194

C

Caesars, the 120

capitalism 150

Cartier 186

Casanova, Giacomo 78-80

channeling 46, 103, 133, 154

children 23, 36-37, 47, 49, 52-53,
    58, 64-65, 68, 77, 85, 107, 118,

L

Lemuria 192
life after death 133, 179
life force 124, 132
life review, the 43, 70, 128, 134-
    136, 138, 150, 159, 194
lightbody 159
lions 36-37, 39, 191, 215
love
    beyond space/time 18, 135, 152,
        179
    love for truth 18, 135
    love seen in all things 18, 90,
        135
    manipulative love 18, 30, 32-33,
        49, 63, 65, 126, 131, 134, 157,
        167, 169-170, 185, 187-189,
        192, 198
    needy love 18, 33, 126, 134, 154,
        184, 188, 194-195, 197, 199
    self love 15, 24, 48, 53, 64, 80,
        138-140, 145-146, 168, 171-
        174, 178, 180, 194, 197, 202,
        204-206, 208-210, 213, 216,
        218, 226
    sexual love 16, 18, 26-27, 31-32,
        36, 39, 76, 98, 113, 121, 126,
        131, 134, 162-163, 167, 169,
        183-184, 188, 191, 195, 205,
        213
    unconditional love 18, 38, 40,

44, 47-48, 64-65, 75, 90, 105,
122, 127, 129-131, 135, 137,
139, 162-164, 166, 170-174,
178, 180, 184, 190, 193-194,
200, 203, 205-206, 208-209,
213-215, 225-226
love yourself into life 27, 200, 207,
    211, 223-224

M

magic 21-22, 25, 27, 77, 90, 108,
    116, 126, 131-132, 134, 141,
    166, 178, 180, 189, 194, 205,
    223
male gender 55, 61
Marie Antoinette 133
marijuana 193
marketing 25, 77
marriage 16, 31, 36, 39, 55, 98,
    101, 107, 114, 126, 131, 153,
    172, 188, 195, 212
Mars 192
masters 16, 18, 51, 53, 58, 60, 62-
    63, 67, 75, 79-80, 103-104,
    111-112, 114-115, 126, 128,
    131, 137, 140, 145, 149-151,
    154, 160, 163, 170, 185, 192,
    208, 218, 223
men 37, 43, 45, 51, 54, 60-61, 66,
    106, 114, 145, 154
menstruation 46, 50, 53

JZK Publishing,
The Library of Ancient Wisdom
A Division of JZK, Inc.
www.jzkpublishing.com

Ramtha, The White Book

General introduction to Ramtha and his teachings.

It addresses questions on the Source of all existence, our forgotten divinity, life after life, evolution, love, the power of consciousness and the mind, lessons from nature, and Ramtha's ascension.

Many people became aware of Ramtha and his teachings in the past through this book.

A Beginner's Guide to Creating Reality,
Revised and Expanded Edition

Account of important events in Ramtha's lifetime, from birth to his ascension, as well as Ramtha's basic teaching on:

- Consciousness and energy
- The nature of reality
- The self and the personality
- The Observer in quantum mechanics
- The auric field surrounding the body
- The kundalini energy, and
- The seven seals in the body

This teaching covers the introduction given to students before commencing studies at Ramtha's School of Enlightenment.

Paperback
Annotated Edition, Glossary, and Index

A Master's Reflection on the History of Humanity
Part I, Human Civilization, Origins and Evolution

This volume tells the story of the origins of humanity before the creation of the physical universe and how we evolved into the first man and woman.

It also describes the genetic manipulation of the human race by other advanced races and how the ancient wisdom of our true origins and nature got lost and buried in superstition and ignorance.

The ancient schools of wisdom preserved the sacred knowledge for a future generation that would be equipped to decipher it and embrace it.

Annotated Edition, Glossary, and Index

A Master's Reflection on the History of Humanity
Part II, Rediscovering the Pearl of Ancient Wisdom

This volume continues the story of the human saga starting with the fall of Atlatia, Ramtha's war, and the fall of women and rising of religion.

It also describes a civilization within the Earth, their UFO connection, and the mystery of the pyramids of Egypt. A central chapter of the book is the story of Pharaoh Ra-Ta-Bin, who was the first human to stand up to the so-called Gods.

The truth about Jehovah, as the God of war and vengeance, is described in great detail. The book closes with Ramtha's description of the next stage in our evolution, the dawn of a new enlightenment.

Annotated Edition, Glossary, and Index

The Mystery of Birth and Death: Redefining the Self

This book explores Ramtha's teachings on the true self, the altered ego, and the mysteries concerning reincarnation and life after death.

Now the teachings of *The Plane of Bliss, Part I,* and *The Plane of Bliss, Part II,* appear together with other key, relevant teachings in one definitive volume.

Some of the subjects discussed in this book are:

- Beginning the path to enlightenment
- The wheel of reincarnation
- The shadow self
- The Egyptian Book of the Dead
- The collapse of human consciousness
- Redefining the self as the spiritual self
- The dark night of the soul
- Death and near-death experiences
- Judgment Day and the life review
- The revelation of our ulterior motives
- The Plane of Bliss and mapping our next lifetime
- Genetics and the soul's journey
- Dimensional mind versus linear mind

Glossary, and Index

The Fireside Series Collection Library

The Fireside Series Collection is an ongoing library of the hottest topics of interest taught by Ramtha. A new book is added every two months.

Paperback
96 pages average, Glossary, Illustrations and Diagrams

Volume One

JZK Publishing
A Division of JZK, Inc.

P.O. Box 1210
Yelm, Washington 98597
360.458.5201
800.347.0439
www.ramtha.com
www.jzkpublishing.com

Made in the USA
Middletown, DE
08 September 2023

37723629R00163